Building Reference Skills in the Elementary School

BUILDING REFERENCE SKILLS IN THE ELEMENTARY SCHOOL

M. ELLEN JAY
HILDA L. JAY

Library Professional Publications
1986

© 1986 M. Ellen Jay and Hilda L. Jay
All rights reserved.
First published 1986 as a Library Professional Publication,
an imprint of The Shoe String Press, Inc.
Hamden, Connecticut 06514

Printed in the United States of America

Library of Congress Cataloging in Publication Data

Jay, M. Ellen.
  Building reference skills in the elementary school.

  Bibliography: p.
  Includes index.
  1. School children—Library orientation. 2. Elementary school libraries—Activity programs. 3. Instructional materials centers—User education. 4. Children's reference books. I. Jay, Hilda L., 1921- . II. Title.
Z675.S3J36   1986   025.5′678′222   86-43
ISBN 0-208-02098-5
ISBN 0-208-02097-7 (pbk.)

Permissions

Citations from the *ASCD Update* (February 1984) quoting Richard Paul, James Howard, Leslie Imel, Anthony Petrosky, and Barry Beyer are reprinted with permission of the Association for Supervision and Curriculum Development. Copyright February 1984 by the Association for Supervision and Curriculum Development. All rights reserved.

Excerpt from *Electricity in Your Life* by Eugene David is reprinted by permission of the publisher, Prentice Hall, Inc., Englewood Cliffs, N.J., 1963.

Excerpts from the Specific Skills Series *Getting the Facts,* including "Clocks, Clocks, Clocks," "They Walk at Night," "No Place Like Home," and "Bells for Ringing" are used by permission of the publisher, Barnell Loft, Ltd., Baldwin, N.Y., 1976.

Excerpts from *Shelf Pets: How to Take Care of Small Wild Animals* by Edward Ricciuti are reprinted by permission of the publisher, Harper and Row, New York, N.Y., 1972.

Excerpts from *Man in Africa* by William Allen are reprinted by permission of the publisher, The Fideler Company, Grand Rapids, Mich., 1981.

Contents

Preface   xi

PART ONE: RATIONALE

Coping with Change   3

The Importance of Thinking Skills   7

Practicing Thinking Skills—A Process Learned in the School Library Media Center   10

Higher Order Intellectual Skills   13

Instructional Philosophy   16

PART TWO: HOW TO USE SPECIFIC REFERENCE TITLES

General Encyclopedias—The First Place to Look   21
    Locating Articles and Gaining Information from Pictures   22
    Locating a Fact   23
    Locating Specific Facts by Key Words   24
    Fact Finding   24
    Compare and Contrast Encyclopedia Coverage   25

Fact Books, Almanacs, and Yearbooks   27
    Famous First Facts   28
    Guinness Book of World Records   29
    Information Please Almanac   30

Specialized Dictionaries   32

Language Arts 33
   Bartlett's Familiar Quotations 35
   Egyptian Hieroglyphs for Everyone 36
   Morris Dictionary of Word and Phrase Origins 37
   Roget's Thesaurus of Words and Phrases 38
   World Mythology Series 39

Science 41
   Grolier's Amazing World of Animals 43
   Let's Discover 44
   Living Earth 45
   Raintree Illustrated Science Encyclopedia 46
   Science and Technology Illustrated 47

Fine Arts 48
   Cathedral 48
   Roofs Over America 49
   World Atlas of Architecture 50
   Young Person's Guide to Ballet 51
   Discovering Art History 52
   Looking at Art: People at Home 53
   Paintings: How to Look at Great Art 54
   Story of American Art for Young People 55
   Home Book of Musical Knowledge 56
   Music Dictionary 57
   What Instrument Shall I Play? 58
   Who's Who in Rock 59
   Rooster's Horns 59
   Encyclopedia of Toys 60

Social Studies and History 62

Chronologies 63
   Who Was When? A Dictionary of Contemporaries 64

Geographical References 66
   Rand McNally Historical Atlas of the World 67
   National Geographic Picture Atlas of Our Fifty States 68
   National Geographic Picture Atlas of Our World 69
   Lands and Peoples 70
   Webster's New Geographical Dictionary 72

Pictorial Histories 74
   Early Settler Life Series 74
   Works of Eric Sloane 75

World History	77
Emergence of Man	77
Encyclopedia of Discovery and Exploration	78
Biographical References	80
Lincoln Library of Sports Champions	82
People Who Made America	83
Something About the Author	83
Webster's Biographical Dictionary	84
Periodicals and Newspapers	87
Collection Development	89
Computer Software—Another Aspect of Collection Development	92

PART THREE: TEACHING THE RESEARCH PROCESS

Effective Instruction	97
Locating Facts	103
Sample Activities for Fact Finding Practice	104
Conflicts: Terminology and Use of Reserves	106
Bibliographies	108
Samples of Text to Use for Bibliography Writing Practice	109
Note Taking Skills	110
1. Note Taking Activity: Four Exercises	112
2. Note Taking Activity: Lizards	115
3. Note Taking Activity: Effects of Regional Differences in Africa	117
4. Note Taking Activity: Astronomy	118
5. Note Taking Activity: What Can Current Do?	120
Organizing Notes	123
Outlining	125
Webbing	126
Flowcharting	128
Revision in the Writing Process	132
Peer Conferencing	135
Checklist	139

PART FOUR: SAMPLE RESEARCH PROJECTS

Curriculum-Related Activities 145
  Short Term Projects 145
    Dinosaurs • Shelters • Rocks and Minerals • Simple 146
    Machines • Human Body • Chemical Elements • Foods
    • Inventions • Sports • Natural Resources • Sound •
    Clocks
  More Complex Projects 151
    Countries • Rivers • Games 151
  Multilevel Adaptations of Projects 153
    Animals • Biographical Research • Black History 153
  A Regularly Scheduled, Integrated, Research-Based
    Discussion Program 158
    Social Studies Enrichment Program (STEP) 159

Bibliography 167

Index 185

Preface

The reader will notice that from time to time activities have been developed based on books that have older copyright dates and may sometimes be out of print. Be aware, therefore, that title choices have not been made solely on the basis of recency of copyright but with other criteria in mind. The authors want the activities to be useful. They have used materials that they found in frequent use in school and public libraries. Quite a period of time often passes before the most recent publications are available in the schools. Moreover, the materials best suited for an age level may not be the newest materials published in the field.

Always, first consideration was given to matching the material with the age level and the curricular content. An effort has been to demonstrate how to stretch the students as much as possible, emphasizing the search process and the use of information found as basic to primary education.

Sometimes consideration was given to size of type. This was true when the suggestion is that the page be photocopied and made into a transparency for projection.

Sometimes the content was the determinant. For example, materials related to colonial foods and cookery are not very plentiful. For this reason the *Little House Cook Book* (1979) is listed in the bibliography as is the more recent *Early Settler Life* series (1981) which has a volume devoted to foods. The school library media and classroom teachers who develop search projects successfully must know the content of the books and other materials in the school library media collection.

Users of this book are always encouraged to make adaptations and to use preferred, more recent or other materials that are available to them. The primary goal is to provide ample and demanding practice in the search process and the use of information as an integrated part of classroom learning activity.

PART ONE
RATIONALE

Coping with Change

There are those who maintain that because of the rapid upsurge of technology, the "old type" library search skills are now all but useless. We certainly have arrived technically at the point where the information anyone needs can be neatly packaged in a database, and with the punching of a few buttons information can be flashed upon a screen or printed out to the user's specifications. Why should valuable classroom time be devoted to the teaching of archaic "library skills?" Some students, hearing these and similar comments regarding the obsolescence rate of information, question whether there is any point in their spending time in classrooms at all. How will they ever use the things they are learning, if, by the time they complete secondary schooling and university experiences, what they have learned will do little to assure them of employment in the real world? So much will have changed that they will have to relearn, if not unlearn, or start anew.

Quite obviously, not everyone subscribes to this extremist view. In fact, expertise in the skills of searching, relating, analyzing and recycling information becomes more vital as the databases become more sophisticated and more fast changing.

The ability to recognize that information is needed, to identify what kind of information it is, to locate sources that include it, to extract from it, and to analyze and evaluate it, as well as to make constructive use of the information, are skills basic to the learning of every person living in the information age. To quote from *Realities: Educational Reform in a Learning Society,* "Our society is characterized by a ceaseless search for solutions to the critical problems that threaten our survival in this age of continuing change. Our learning society is also an information-based society. Each person needs the means to cope with the magnitude of data currently being generated."[1]

Educators, struggling with reassessing the validity of educational goals and the uncertainty of the future for which they are attempting to prepare students, have concluded that the traditional approach to learning facts needs overhauling. Emphases require adjustment. To this extent, they and their students are seeing things the same way.

The literature is overflowing with commentary on the dilemmas associated with attempting to prepare today's young people to cope with a changed tomorrow. Carl R. Rogers maintains that

> If our present culture survives, it will be because we have been able to develop individuals for whom change is the central facet of life and who have been able to live comfortably with this central fact. It means that they will not be concerned, as so many are today, that their past learning is inadequate to enable them to cope with current situations. They will instead have the comfortable expectation that it will be continuously necessary to incorporate new and challenging learnings about ever-changing situations.[2]

Typical of the conclusions of many of the writers is John Goodlad's comment made in *A Place Called School*. He writes, "The ultimate effect would be, of course, that all students would have experienced, by the time of graduation, a curricular core. I argue against a common set of topics constituting this core but for a common set of concepts, principles, skills, and ways of knowing."[3]

This is not as abrupt a philosophical shift as it might at first seem. The American people have long been identified by their interest in information. Schooling for everyone, the enduring popularity of periodicals and newspapers, the widespread use of television and radio for instant information, and the fascination with ever-advancing communications technology have set us apart in the world. Our school curricula planners have shown a preference for teaching/learning based not on the lecture notes regurgitated on tests, but on learning which requires thinking and fewer "right" and "wrong" answers. Students are encouraged to examine information, develop views of their own, and support and defend them. They are taught to respect differences of opinion, the right of others to think their own thoughts. Indeed, the Constitution of the United States protects this right. It should follow naturally that because our students must be taught to think, the basic curriculum required of every student include "thinking skills."

The school library media center and its program of curricular use are essential to providing basic educational opportunity for American children. The ideas that "good schools require good school libraries,"[4] or that every teacher has a responsibility to help students become more skilled in the use of information sources are not new. It is becoming increasingly apparent, however, that in a period of rapid change virtually the only sound approach to the education of the young is to make sure they have the best possible thinking skills and the finest ability possible to locate and effectively use information. And paired with this realization comes one just as logical, that "library research and information skills be taught as a new basic—providing instruction within the library program and in all subject areas at each level of elementary and secondary school."[5]

Perhaps the student need, school responsibility, and classroom problems regarding the teaching/learning of search skills has been stated best by a graduate student enrolled in a reference course. She was writing a reaction report to a current journal article on the use of reference books in schools. Portions of her reaction report follow:

> The author of this article thinks that students need to be made familiar early in their careers with techniques for getting the most out of a library. Students, even when formally introduced to a library, rarely receive the kind of detailed instruction in library skills which will enable them to use a library to its capacity.
>
> I am living proof of this author's words. I have always been a model student, a regular library patron and have worked in both a public library and a college library; yet until this course I did not know the first thing about really tapping a library's resources. I now know how valuable such instruction can be . . .
>
> There is need for closer cooperation between teachers and librarians. I am struck by a lack of cooperation between the two. That lack, I suspect, stems from the relative ignorance of the teachers about what libraries offer. If teachers go through college the way I did, never receiving adequate instruction in the use of the libraries, then of course they will not be able to guide their students in using the library. If teachers are not aware enough of their deficiencies in teaching their students how to use the library, then librarians must take the initiative and make their presence felt—firmly and convincingly.[6]

Notes

1. American Library Association Task Force on Excellence in Education, *Realities: Educational Reform in a Learning Society* (Chicago: American Library Association, 1984), 7.

2. Quoted in *A Guide to School Library Media Programs* (Hartford: Connecticut State Department of Education, 1982), Preface.

3. Quoted in *A Report of a Task Force on Higher Order Intellectual Skills* (Rockville, Md.: Montgomery County Public Schools, 1984), 6.

4. American Library Association, *Realities,* 4.

5. Ibid., 6.

6. Christina Hartmayer, *"Reaction Report #10"* (Class work for ESIM 340, Reference and Information Services, University of Connecticut, 1985), 1–2.

The Importance of Thinking Skills

Research tells us that thinking skills can be upgraded and honed. As a result, many school systems have instituted special programs for various groups of students in an effort to make certain that proper emphasis is placed on improving these skills. The terminology varies as widely as the program approaches themselves. In the literature, one reads of "decision making," "problem solving," "critical thinking," "thinking skills," "higher order intellectual skills," "talented and gifted" opportunities. Not only computer software designers, but also summer camp directors and many others who sell services for children have become aware of the interest in, and the emphasis being placed on these skills. Both the schools and individual parents seek out and purchase for their children materials purported to enhance these skills.

Major national reports, such as that of the National Assessment Project and *A Nation at Risk,* support the need, either directly or indirectly, to place increased emphasis on teaching "thinking" skills. To illustrate how much attention is being given to improving students' thought processes, consider what a number of educators from various parts of the United States and representatives of all levels of schools have written in the *ASCD Update* (February 1984) regarding this concern.

Richard Paul, director of the Center for Critical Thinking and Moral Critique, Sonoma State University, Calif. believes one should understand critical thinking as being composed of "rock bottom skills for a comprehensive approach in which autonomous questioning, reasoned judgment, and reciprocity are encouraged in the fullest degree."[7]

James Howard, consultant on the teaching of writing skills, Westport, Mass. writes:

> Writing is much more than an aggregate of communications skills. It is a basic discipline of learning, a technology of thinking. Any worthwhile writing assignment leaves students to the solitude of their own minds, where they must sort out what they have been taught, what they have read, what they have experienced or even imagined. Having sorted out, they must select and put some of all that together in a relationship that has meaning . . .
>
> Translated into the terminology of "higher order skills," this sorting and putting together becomes "data-gathering, synthesizing and problem solving." Even the narratives children write in the early grades of school require such skills in some degree, and if writing were part of the familiar routine of schooling in every subject in every grade, students would graduate from high school with well-developed thinking skills.[8]

Leslie Imel, principal of Sunset Elementary School, Lawrence, Calif., has this to say:

> Thinking skills can be improved if and when a school wants to make them important and provide help in carrying them out. . . . Good questions can be practiced in all subject areas and at all age levels. With in-service training and a clear plan of responsibility, we developed a curriculum model with five major components: classifying, organizing, problem solving, making reasoned judgments, and identifying alternate points of view. . . . Thinking skills are beginning to take priority in many or our lessons.[9]

Both Anthony Petrosky and Barry Beyer, theorists on thinking, concur that thinking skills will be improved when they are intermixed with regular, ongoing curriculum.[10] This is of particular importance to school library media teachers who have shown repeatedly that library skills are not thoroughly learned and assimilated when they are segregated from everyday usage. They develop best when they are integrated into the daily classroom activity and assignments in all subject areas.

Evaluation tools designed for use by accrediting agencies and by the state departments of education in states where use of the school library media center is considered an important teaching element contain at least one evaluative measure in which the words *integrated* and *program* are related to the school library media center. There appears to be increasing interest in identifying research which has shown the value of the school library media *program* in education. The word *program* is emphasized here because materials, space, and personnel can be in place and still produce no program to engage the students. It is an interaction of minds and information that must take place in order to produce *program*.

If it is apparent that activities to require thinking skills must be integrated into ongoing classroom instruction and that the school library media center program can be of value in providing thinking skills practice, then it follows logically that the school library media center program and the classroom instructional program must be closely integrated if the best opportunities are to be offered to the students.

Notes

7. *ASCD Update* (Alexandria, Va.: Association for Supervision and Curriculum Development, February 1984), 4.

8. Ibid., 4.

9. Ibid., 5.

10. *Report of a Task Force on Higher Order Intellectual Skills* (Rockville, Md.: Montogomery County Public Schools, 1984), 10.

Practicing Thinking Skills—
A Process Learned in the School
Library Media Center

The relationship between thinking skills and the school library media center program has a lengthy history. In May 1966, Frances Henne observed that there was a school of thought among media specialists that the library skills generally being taught were not entirely on target. "In the view of many school librarians the mere process of locating and finding materials in the library holds little intellectual benefit for students, and time thus spent is generally wasted time. The many processes involved in what students do with materials—evaluation, synthesis, reflection, thinking, appreciation, or whatever—are the important factors, not the searching, locating, and assembling of materials."[11]

Granted, the student who can enter the school library media center, use the indexing tools, follow the locater clues, and proceed to put hands on needed materials is going to move far ahead of the student who has to stand in line asking for help with these basics. The materials that student needs may have been picked up and checked out, and will be contributing to someone else's paper before there is a chance to obtain the library media teacher's attention.

The more technically aware students who expect to use a database before (or without) consulting available in-house references, place themselves at the mercy of the abstracter or indexer who stocked the database. Just as using only a single authority for source information subjects one to bias, so does using any material mindlessly. Total acceptance of another's thinking can lead to manipulation.

However, there seems to be an increasing realization that what Henne and her colleagues were saying then still has merit. It is not enough to have materials at hand, although that is an essential element. The classroom teacher and the school library media teacher must accept a shared responsibility to provide the students with experiences with materials that tend to increase their thinking powers.

It has long been recognized that the classroom teacher is the greatest force in influencing the students' use of the school media center. The topic has been the subject of countless studies and the findings have always indicated that classroom teachers, through their chosen style of teaching, their lesson designs, and their private convictions about the worth of school library media center usage exert a major influence over students' attitudes toward the center.

A school library media specialist who is aware of this, who has classroom teaching background or experience, who makes the classroom teacher using the school library media center as a teaching tool feel comfortable and supported, who teams with the classroom teacher and shares the instructional role, will undoubtedly be able to "influence the influencer." To the extent that there is understanding and acceptance by both the classroom teacher and the school library media specialist of their professional responsibilities, and to the extent that both are committed to use of the center as a teaching/learning tool, student ability to make the most of the school library media center for learning will improve.

When the approach in the classroom is textbook-bound, when the teacher is the principal interpreter of information, when the instructional method is largely expository, school library media center activity will be scarce indeed. On the other hand, when the instructional mode emphasises inquiry, the use of multiple sources of information, and questioning, and when the teacher places high value on the students' thought processes, a learning process is in place which *requires* the extensive use of a school library media center.

Just as the classroom teacher must move out of traditional textbook and lecture-oriented presentation methods, so the school library media teacher must move out of the traditional "library skills" lessons approach. Emphasis shifts to devising learning centers and creating, both with and for the classroom teacher, projects that stretch the students' horizons and give them a chance to learn to search for resources and use processes that are fundamental to the learning of higher order intellectual skills.

Notes

11. Frances Henne, "As Good as Librarians Make Them," *School Libraries* 15 May 1966: 2565.
12. Montgomery County Public Schools, *Report,* 12.
13. Ibid., 16.

Higher Order Intellectual Skills

What is the basis of the compatability of learning higher order intellectual skills and learning to do effective information searches in school or other library media centers? According to one definition:

> Higher order intellectual skills are those mental processes, including critical and creative thinking, which go beyond recall and rote learning and require the individual to use inductive, deductive, and/or analogical reasoning. These higher order intellectual skills are characterized by the depth of processing, the complexity of concepts and generalizations formed, and the monitoring of the entire thinking processes.[12]

Students must make choices when they have a wide variety of materials from which to select those most appropriate for their needs. They must evaluate the sources, they must read with comprehension, they must analyze, and finally synthesize. The classroom and school library media teachers become guides, coordinators of discussions, and managers of the learning experience. The search for needed information takes on inquiry aspects. Questions are raised and the possible answers are sought. A problem-solving orientation is established. The student is forced to use mental facilities at a more demanding level than when texts and lectures are accepted unquestioningly.

Under these conditions the center and the school library media teacher take on substantially more importance in the education process. Working as a team, the classroom and school library media teachers, give the students more stimulation and assistance. They may provide shared classroom instruction and/or individual assistance; the two together have been shown to develop increased problem-solving abilities in the students. Whereas the school library media center was formerly looked upon as useful in a supplemental/supportive role, it now serves as an active part of the entire teaching/learning process.

There have been studies made to identify the classroom environment which fosters competency in higher order intellectual skills. Often there are commonalities found among schools of recognized excellence. These include teacher enthusiasm, active and responsible participation by students, both encouragment of and respect for divergent thinking, the use of many and varied materials, and a constant effort on the part of the teachers to upgrade their own information and skills. When these attributes are compared with those considered indicative of a good school library media center atmosphere, there are, not surprisingly, consistent similarities.

A Task Force on Higher Order Intellectual Skills included the following list of elements to be developed in classrooms fostering higher order intellectual skills:

Students are actively involved.
Individual differences are respected and addressed.
Self-direction and independence are encouraged.
Tangential thinking is accepted.
Challenging activities and materials are provided and thinking is stimulated.
Risk-taking is allowed.
Ideas are valued.
Affective and social needs are considered.
Experimenting with ideas is encouraged.
Intellectual playfulness is permitted.
Interaction and communication are encouraged.
Ideas are accepted and constructively judged.
Structure appropriate to the task is planned.

The teacher who is a critical and creative thinker, who is confident in the process and structure for developing higher order intellectual skills, and willing to foster this classroom environment within the structure of curriculum, will do most to promote growth of higher order intellectual skills in students.[13]

When there are two mutually reinforcing elements—two teachers, (classroom and library media) and two physical areas, (the classroom and the school library media center), the students receive at least twice the amount of help and opportunity to grow in independence.

If competency in using and processing knowledge is now a universal need, and if solving problems and making decisions are a part of everyone's life both at home and on the job, then the school opportunities for acquiring these skills should be just as universal. The strategies that have been identified as effective in developing higher order intellectual skills need to be known and practiced by every teacher. There is mounting evidence that these skills can and should be learned early and need to be practiced throughout the elementary school grades. The school library media center is a proven laboratory for their implementation for *every* child, and this underscores heavily the joint responsibilities of the classroom and the school library media teachers.

In schools that are seeking to improve their level of excellence through upgrading student opportunity to experience and practice "thinking," a genuine reevaluation of the school library media center program could prove fruitful. This reevaluation should review actual performance as well as potentials. Good school library media centers—suitably staffed, readily accessible, sufficiently spacious to accommodate varied and balanced collections, and the activity generated by the classroom demands—are invaluable to the learning process. When investment in the center is looked upon as costly (or as an optional or even extravagant use of public funds), it usually follows that the school library media center program is not suitably developed or fully integrated into the daily learning process. When the school library media center program is an integral part of the curriculum, teachers, students, and each subject area gain from its services, materials, and opportunities. Once students have acquired the ability to locate information, and tasted the satisfactions of using that information for their own purposes, there are few limits; any subject area may be explored. A basic equity is established among all students once they have learned to locate and use information independently. Satisfied interests spawn new ones; an expanded self-concept fed by success enhances student motivation.

Instructional Philosophy

Any school system that wants to assure effective educational opportunity for its students should develop specific statements of goals and of objectives within the framework of what the educational community is trying to achieve collectively. These goals statements should include references to the use of the school library media center. Like all statements of policy, these goals and objectives will be reevaluated and revised from time to time. Student achievement, teacher performance, and stated objectives all deserve scrutiny as they relate and interact upon each other.

To assure as much variety and equality of learning opportunity as possible, officially designed and approved curricula must incorporate use of learning skills in such a way that they require teacher and student familiarity with, and constant use of, the materials from the school library media center. When development and use of such skills are an integral part of the curriculum, supervisory administrators must accept responsibility for including the use of the school library media center as a teaching/learning tool as one measure of their faculty evaluations. Evaluation forms should include a section addressing this function of classroom teaching. The school system may wish to use a library and study skills achievement test that has been designed in-house, or a standardized one. Usually the in-house product reflects more accurately the goals of the school and the materials the students have been using. The segments of standardized tests (such as the Iowa or California tests) that address study and thought skills can be valued assessments of student achievement in these areas as well. One thing is quite certain: if supervisory administrators recognize the importance of the students' library as a learning/teaching tool by making these a specific part of each teacher's evaluation, more attention will be focused on these skills. What is emphasized as being important in the evaluation will be reflected in the classroom activity.

The school library media teacher and the classroom teacher form a team. Together they individualize and personalize—even customize—instructional units in such a manner that exposure to curricular content stresses learning the skills that permit continuous student growth. To achieve the ability to manipulate information effectively and to process it with higher order thinking, relating and extrapolating patterns, is basic among educational goals, and essential in coping with change. The crowning achievement is to develop the ability to communicate the product of this information processing to others.

These skills can not be learned in isolation. They require practice and integration into the everyday ongoing classroom activity. They can not be an "add-on" to the already overcrowded school day; they must be an integral part of classroom activities and expectations. In this way, not only is more accomplished in the same amount of time, but purpose and meaning is enhanced.

The school library media center is as much a learning center as is a classroom. The school library media teacher is a fully functioning member of the teaching faculty. Certification for these specialists includes courses in educational theory, methods, and practice teaching, as well as courses in library procedures and services. These specialized courses build expertise in reference skills, children's literature, selection of materials, audiovisual materials design and preparation, as well as cataloging and organizing techniques, and administration of a school library media center collection and equipment.

The school library media center belongs to everyone in the school and especially to the students. Sometimes a center has been looked upon as the "possession" of the librarian. When this happens the basic integration of the center into learning activity tends to be missing. Only with intermeshing and cooperating will the center's fullest educational contribution be achieved.

Too often skills programs in lower grades tend to stop with the location of materials. Worse still, this activity takes place in the form of discussion or pencil and paper quizzes. Students are often able to say that fiction is shelved alphabetically by the author's last name, but they will continue to ask, "Where are the mysteries?" They can not *apply* what they respond to accurately on a quiz.

Sometimes worksheets, if they are used at all, require every student to answer the same question the same way. When every student is asked to answer questions which result in identical answers, minimal learning takes place. When questions are worded in such a way that individual answers are unique because they relate to a specific member of a category, students are challenged. For example, if the students are asked to find the population of a city, they should each be assigned different cities or at least cities beginning with a different letter in order to control choice of city names used.

When commercial materials are used, this individualization is often absent. When a mock-up instead of the actual reference tool (e.g., a picture of fronts of catalog drawers) is substituted, the students are cheated of real demonstration or hands-on experiences. Also, there is a possibility that the material referred to is not in the local collection or does not make use of the challenging items that are in some stronger collections.

When such limited skills are the only ones addressed for six years it is no wonder that students become negatively attuned to the school library media center. Not only does unapplied repetition of highly similar short answer and multiple choice quizzes contribute to boredom, they also strongly suggest that their content covers all there is to know about using a library effectively.

Students are ready for much more. First grade students can begin to identify facts successfully, yet many older students demonstrate difficulty with this task. Most students are assisted significantly by structured classroom instruction in search and use skills. There needs to be continuous and expanding instruction in how to use the materials once they are found, how to evaluate findings, and how to organize the presentation of one's thoughts about these findings. These skills can be acquired only through frequent, varied, and integrated hands-on types of experiences. To be truly effective, these lesson activities must be skillfully tailored to match ongoing classroom activity. The success of the library media skills program is dependent upon a schoolwide sense of responsibility and collaboration.

PART TWO
HOW TO USE SPECIFIC REFERENCE TITLES

General Encyclopedias—
The First Place to Look

General encyclopedias provide a good resource for the earliest search experiences. The broad coverage of topics headed with nouns or substantive phrases and arranged alphabetically provides basic information quickly and easily.

Headings are abstract nouns such as art, music, or mythology. Most are names of things such as animals, insects, money, or transportation. Others are proper names of persons, countries, states, wars, or periods of time. Some information on a topic is printed under a related heading in another volume, and so the index must be used to find complete information contained in an encyclopedia.

An encyclopedia has its limitations. It is not possible to cover all the information of the world in some thirty volumes. The editors will have had to develop a coverage and inclusion policy; therefore, even general encyclopedias will have leanings toward certain areas of information or specialities. There should be several different encyclopedia titles in the collection because each will prove superior in some respect to other encyclopedia publications. And of course, due to the production time lag, no encyclopedia is able to include the events of the year of its (or its yearbooks') publication.

Learning activities devised in terms of general encyclopedias should include alphabetizing (sometimes by word), decoding of abbreviations, cross-referencing, use of subheadings, skimming skills, fact finding, notetaking—but not necessarily in that order. Students need to appreciate that the general encyclopedia is a proper first stop for learning enough about a topic to use other more specialized references for finding additional information.

Most multivolume encyclopedias are now published with a cumulative index in a separate volume. Some, like *Compton's* and *Book of Knowledge,* have end-of-volume indexes as well as the final volume, cumulative index. For individual reference the added end-of-volume indexes do not make too much difference, but for classroom instruction and practice, having the extra indexes can be useful. Occasionally, a juvenile encyclopedia is published without an index. Although the reference may be useful and interesting for a browser, it is not well suited for the type of learning activities that call for the use of an index. In fact, its use can be somewhat counterproductive if the aim is to ingrain the habitual use of an index to obtain all information on the topic sought from a multivolume set.

ENCYCLOPEDIA WORKSHEET 1: LOCATING ARTICLES AND GAINING INFORMATION FROM PICTURES

1. Look up CAT
   On what page does the information start? _____
   Name one thing a cat is doing in a picture on that page.

   ---

2. Look up FIRE
   On what page does the information start? _____
   Name one method of starting a fire pictured there.

   ---

3. Look up HOUSE
   On what page does the information start? _____
   Name one kind of house pictured there.

   ---

4. Look up LIBRARY
   On what page does the information start? _____
   What do you see people doing in the picture?

   ---

5. Look up MONEY
   On what page does the information start? _____
   Name some object that has been used for money.

   ---

6. Look up PAINTING
   On what page does the information start? _____
   Name something you see in a painting pictured on this page.
   _____

7. Look up TEXAS
   On what page does the information start? _____
   What is the nickname of the state of Texas?
   _____

ENCYCLOPEDIA WORKSHEET 2: LOCATING A FACT

DIRECTIONS: Look up each of the topics listed below. Read the entry. Find one fact. Write it in your own words. DO NOT COPY. Include the volume and page numbers where you found the fact.

1. AGOUTI. Vol. _____ Page _____
   Fact _____

2. DELTA. Vol. _____ Page _____
   Fact _____

3. GINGHAM. Vol. _____ Page _____
   Fact _____

4. NETTLE. Vol. _____ Page _____
   Fact _____

5. PIPIT. Vol. _____ Page _____
   Fact _____

6. QUOITS. Vol. _____ Page _____
   Fact _____

7. SCALP. Vol. _____ Page _____
   Fact _____

8. TRUFFLE. Vol. _____ Page _____
   Fact _____

9. VELVET. Vol. _____ Page _____
   Fact _____

10. ZINC. Vol. _____ Page _____
    Fact _____

ENCYCLOPEDIA WORKSHEET 3: LOCATING SPECIFIC FACTS BY KEY WORDS

DIRECTIONS: Read each question. Find the key word. Look it up. Write the answer to the question.

1. What does BAMBOO look like?

2. How many DOMINOES are there in a set?

3. What are the HIMALAYAS?

4. What do MAYAPPLE leaves look like?

5. What are ORCHIDS?

6. What other bird does the RHEA look like?

7. How many permanent TEETH does a person have?

8. Where does WOOL come from?

HINT: For this activity use one of the following encyclopedias: *Worldbook, Britannica Jr., Compton's,* or *Book of Knowledge* (for some questions only). Write the encyclopedia title used in abbreviated form (W, JR, C, or BK) and the page number where you found your answer after your answer in the blank. This will help if you need to go back and check the answers.

ENCYCLOPEDIA WORKSHEET 4: FACT FINDING

DIRECTIONS: Choose a topic card. Locate the topic. Note the topic, volume, and pages used, and write the answer to the question in the spaces provided on the answer sheet.

1. Looked up _____ Vol. _____ Page _____
   Answer _____

2. Looked up _____ Vol. _____ Page _____
   Answer _____

3. Looked up _____ Vol. _____ Page _____
   Answer _____

SAMPLE TOPIC CARD FORMAT:

1. Look up LITHOGRAPHY   Vol.?   Page?
   Where, when, and by whom was the process invented?

2. Look up FOSSIL   Vol.?   Page?
   How are fossils made?

3. Look up GLASS   Vol.?   Page?
   Of what is glass made?

4. Look up RAINBOW   Vol.?   Page?
   Name three places you can see a rainbow.

5. Look up ECLIPSE   Vol.?   Page?
   When will the next solar eclipse occur?

NOTE TO TEACHER: As many searches can be asked for as the teacher desires. If there are significantly more topic cards than students, or more questions than students are required to answer, students may choose the questions that interest them the most. Or, they may be instructed to take the front card, answer the question, and return the card to the back of the file when they are finished with it.

ENCYCLOPEDIA WORKSHEET 5: COMPARE AND CONTRAST ENCYCLOPEDIA COVERAGE

ASSIGNED TOPIC: _____

1. How many pages of information would you find if you went directly to the volume without using the index?
   Encyclopedia #1 _____ Pages _____
   Encyclopedia #2 _____ Pages _____
   Encyclopedia #3 _____ Pages _____

2. How many pages of information would you find if you followed the leads in the index?

Encyclopedia #1 _____ Pages _____
Encyclopedia #2 _____ Pages _____
Encyclopedia #3 _____ Pages _____

3. How many different volumes contain information related to your topic?
   Encyclopedia #1 _____ Vols. _____
   Encyclopedia #2 _____ Vols. _____
   Encyclopedia #3 _____ Vols. _____

4. Which encyclopedia provides you with the most information about your topic? Encyclopedia #_____. Pages _____
   Entries: _____
   Special features: _____
   _____

Fact Books, Almanacs, and Yearbooks

Yearbooks, as their name implies, are annual publications. They are sometimes called fact books, and because of their broad coverage of topics tend to be kept in a "ready reference" collection rather than being placed with a particular subject section of the collection. On the other hand, yearbooks published to update general encyclopedias will probably be kept with the encyclopedia.

The student learns that yearbooks provide the most up-to-date information in book form. In retrospect they provide a record of an entire year's events. They tend to be assembled in unpredictable arrangements and use of the index is entirely necessary for finding information—unless the purpose, as with an almanac, may be merely to browse for fun.

Government publications such as the handbooks published by each state fall into the yearbooks classification. So does the *Statistical Abstract of the United States,* although this is not a publication that would get tremendous use in an elementary school collection. For the comparison of prices over the years and such things as immigration statistics, which do prove useful, *Historical Statistics of the United States, Colonial Times to 1970* is invaluable.

Among the popular fact books are the annual almanacs, especially *World Almanac and Book of Facts* and *Information Please Almanac. Famous First Facts* and the *Guinness Book of World Records* are also very popular, although not annuals. All provide ready access to innumerable amounts of assorted information.

Because of this, they are especially useful as starting points for beginning searchers.

■ FAMOUS FIRST FACTS (4th ed. rev., 1981)

Contents of book:

American firsts. Some nine thousand inventions, discoveries, and happenings since the arrival of the Vikings in the year 1007.

Useful characteristics:

Five separate indexes permit access by topic (alphabetic), by person involved (alphabetic), by geographic location (alphabetic lists by state, subdivided by towns), by year, and by day of the year. The topic entry is the main entry. The other indexes are cross-referenced to the topic index so that complete information may be found easily.

Skills involved:

1. Realizing that a book may contain multiple indexes and locating the appropriate one. The index at the back of the book is only one of five. When there are multiple indexes, only one index contains complete information. This is referred to as the main entry.
2. Locating the entry within the index using either alphabetic or chronological order.
3. Moving from cross-reference entries to main entry to acquire full information if needed.
4. Interpreting the meanings of bold face and regular typeface entries.

Developing activities:

1. Using the month and day (not necessarily the year) of the student's birthday, select a favorite "first" that occurred on that date. Use the index by years to select another "first" for the same year. Using the town of residence, home town, or a town within one's state, select a favorite "first" for that location. Using the names index, select a favorite "first" accomplished by an individual whose last initial is the same as the student's.
2. The students should write down the information needed to

lead them to the main entry. This information appears in boldface type (which is the topic term), and is followed by additional qualifying information needed to identify a specific entry among others on the same topic.
3. Identify the what, the who, the where, and the when for each of the firsts selected.
4. For any unit of study, students could be asked to create a timeline of famous firsts related to the subject. Particularly appropriate might be transportation, communications, or inventions that fostered the industrial revolution.
5. When studying the history and geography of your state create a timeline or a map showing locations labeled with important firsts.
6. Pick a month and identify the famous firsts that occurred and create a calendar that includes this information.
7. Identify the event and give the details described for the earliest event listed. (This is the birth of Snorro, the first child of European parents born in America. Thorsinn Karlsefni was his father and Gudrid, widow of Leif Ericsson's brother, was his mother. In time he returned to Iceland and became important in government there.)

■ GUINNESS BOOK OF WORLD RECORDS (1982)

Contents of book:

Lists record-setting accomplishments worldwide, and is organized into twelve categories. Table of contents lists categories and subdivisions thereof; index lists specific terms related to the records.

Useful characteristics:

1. High interest.
2. Short entries.
3. Illustrated.
4. Readable.
5. Indexed.
6. Contains table of contents.

Skills involved:

1. Alphabetizing.
2. Locating term in an index.

3. Turning to appropriate page.
4. Finding entry on page.
5. Locating fact within the entry.

Developing activities:

1. Start by using the index. Choose terms related to subjects being studied or topics of interest. If one were doing a unit on climate, select a term such as *desert*. Turn to the page listed (156) and find the entry *Largest desert*. Given the information provided, the simplest question would be to ask for the name of the largest desert in the world. More experienced students could be asked how much of the world's land surface is considered to be desert, or to infer the annual amount of rainfall that constitutes desert conditions. Similar questions could be developed using index terms such as rainfall, temperature, snowfall, flood, fogs, wind, etc.
2. Before launching a letter-writing activity with pen pals, the following questions could be explored: What is the longest pen pal writing relationship on record? When did it occur? Who was involved? By looking up the term "pen pals" in the index, one is led to an entry (p. 226) labeled "Most Durable Pen Pals."
3. Additional practice could be obtained by using fun-type entries such as yo-yo; domino toppling; bubble gum blowing; or camel, roasted. The range is almost limitless.
4. It should be noted that the Guinness records are published in a ten volume series called *Guinness Illustrated Collection of World Records for Young People*. Any title in this series could be used as the resource for similar activities.

■ INFORMATION PLEASE ALMANAC

Contents of book:

Miscellaneous facts and figures, both current and retrospective, including people and places, dates and data, current events, nutrition, sports, science, education, energy, entertainment, and much more.

Useful characteristics:

1. Index.
2. Special articles related to the year of publication.

Skills involved:

1. Ability to use the index.
2. Interpretation of charts and statistical information (using headings accurately).
3. Abbreviations.
4. Alternative terminology.

Developing activities:

1. Look for animal group terminology in the index. Find the group name for selected animals such as, a *drift* of hogs, a *bed* of oysters, or a *pod* of seals.
2. Find statistics relating to the Statue of Liberty and the text of Emma Lazarus's, "The New Colossus."
3. Find out who holds the record for catching a large-mouthed bass with a rod and reel. Indicate the index term used to find the information as well as the statistics regarding the catch.
4. Find out what is meant by the following terms of measurement: *bale, hand, knot, stone,* and *quire*.
5. Find out the following "firsts" associated with aviation: parachute jump, U.S. woman pilot, jet liner service.
6. Find out how to address a letter to Queen Elizabeth II; to President Reagan; to the governor of your state.

Specialized Dictionaries

It is a toss-up whether specialized dictionaries or general encyclopedias are the better first stop for information. Each gives the background information needed to launch a full-fledged search on a particular topic. Because specialized references are usually arranged or limited by a date span, a geographic area, or a professional or disciplinary theme, this basic information is needed to locate the proper source of additional information. Specialized dictionaries (sometimes called handbooks) provide this information, as well as names of persons involved or related to the topic, in rather brief entries.

For this reason, specialized dictionaries may be used by students younger than the editors probably had in mind. It should be understood that it is not necessary to be able to read every word in an article in order to pick out needed facts. On occasion, an entry might be read to a student since children can often understand vocabulary they are not yet able to read for themselves.

Specialized dictionaries are prepared for almost every field. They traditionally use alphabetic arrangement, usually the letter-by-letter system, although some handbooks use the word-by-word system. Revising editions calls for adding material. It also means dropping material found in an earlier reference. Therefore, it may be useful to consult more than one edition of a dictionary or handbook, just as one does with the yearbooks. Placement or use of the specialized dictionary would depend upon its level. There are some quite simple ones such as *Dinosaur Dictionary* by Glut or *Music Dictionary* by Davis.

Activities designed for use of handbooks and specialized dictionaries will involve mainly alphabetizing and fact finding.

Language Arts

Foreign languages are taught in some elementary schools as a part of the standard curriculum. In other schools, refugee or other immigrant children make languages an important consideration. Additionally, foreign words appear in stories, magazine articles, or news reports with international emphases. These words are not aways explained in the text. There should be, therefore, foreign language dictionaries available so that the meanings of the terms can be identified.

There should be a variety of English language dictionaries on hand to serve different levels of expertise. And when there are students learning English as a second language in the school, bilingual dictionaries are essential.

The beginning reader is concentrating on basic word attack skills. Initially, decoding the sound symbols leads to recognizing familiar words for which meaning is already known. As the reader progresses, the word may be decoded, but its meaning may still be unknown. Where do they go from here? The better readers and writers increase their vocabulary and word choice. They recognize subtle differences in meanings and enjoy a play on words. The introduction of a wide variety of language references helps to establish an interest in words.

Specialized dictionaries emphasize prefixes, suffixes, root words; origins and derivations; synonyms, homonyms, antonyms. There is so much more depth and range to be explored in them than in an unabridged dictionary.

Specialized language dictionaries include such useful types as a thesaurus; a dictionary of synonyms and antonyms; or books of word and phrase origins, of prefixes and suffixes, of clichés, and of pronunciation; and especially the little gem known as a "word book." Word books usually provide only spelling, syllable division, and accent marks. One of the simplest is *Spellex Word Finder,* which groups all variations with the base word rather than placing them in a strictly alphabetic arrangement. For the child who resists using a dictionary to verify spelling, the word book is a genuine miracle. Not enough use is made of them.

Much of the reference material used in an elementary school depends on the curriculum. Language arts include fiction, short stories, drama, poetry, folklore, mythology, speech, slang, vocabulary development, word derivation, word and phrase origin, quotations, spelling, and grammar. There is great variation among schools as to which of these facets of language arts receives extensive attention. Some get only a passing nod, but even so, reference materials are needed for them, too.

Another use of the term "word book" is in referring to such books as Joan Hanson's series which—incidentally—set some kind of record for long subtitles. For example, there is *Antonym: Hot and Cold and Other Words That Are As Different as Night and Day,* or *Homographs: Bow and Bow and Other Words That Look the Same but Sound as Different as Sow and Sow,* and so on. What school could be without these? And then there is a book such as *I Hear America Talking* that provides interesting background about where our words came from, origins that are often tied into American history. Other series that are done well are those by Funk such as *Hog on Ice,* or *Horsefeathers,* and those done by Asimov bearing titles such as *Words on the Map* or *Words from the Myths,* or *Words of Science.* Also useful is the three volume set called *Morris Dictionary of Word and Phrase Origins.* These identify the origin of a word or phrase meaning, as opposed to derivation.

Books of quotations and proverbs have a place in the collection. *Bartlett's Familiar Quotations* holds on to its long-established popularity. Proverbs will be found in references devoted to this particular type of quotation and the title of the book usually contains the word "proverbs." More modern quotations will be found in quotation books bearing more recent copyright dates. Young people need to learn that the quotations chosen for any collection are selected by the editor, just as are collections of poems or stories, and that if one book does not contain a desired quotation, another book of quotations very well might. The concept of the term "concordance" is worth knowing. It is not necessary to know the beginning of a quotation; a fragment will do. Then, using the *key words* of the fragment and the concordance as an index, a quotation may be identified from a number of different access points.

When poetry receives a good deal of attention, consideration should be given to providing a poetry index. Brewton's *Index to Poetry for Children and Young People* and Smith and Andrews's *Subject Index to Poetry for Children and Young People* are more oriented toward children's poetry than is *Granger's Index to Poetry.* If fairy tales, myths, and legends also receive attention, an index is helpful. Ireland's index is more recent than Eastman's. *Funk & Wagnalls Standard Dictionary of Folklore, Mythology, and Legend* is helpful in explaining symbolism. *Brewer's Dictionary of Phrase and Fable* and *The Reader's Encyclopedia* are basic to any collection. Their use in explaining allusions from art, music, geography, and history, in addition to many facets of literature, make them essential. Because of their short entries, these adult books are good ones for younger students to start with, provided they have guidance in doing so.

■ BARTLETT'S FAMILIAR QUOTATIONS (14th ed., 1968)*

Contents of book:

Quotations, identified by author and source, arranged chronologically under 2,250 authors' names. Key word index (concordance) permits identification of quotations "inadequately remembered." Quotations are representative of scientific and technological fields, politics, and the classics and include some from Far Eastern cultures.

Useful characteristics:

1. The chronological arrangement permits examination of ideas in the context of their period.
2. All quotes for a given author are grouped together.
3. Separate author index assists locating author's quotations within chronological listing.
4. Concordance index permits locating a quotation that includes a specific word.

Skills involved:

1. Alphabetizing.
2. Chronological arrangement.
3. Difference between being an author and being a subject of a quotation.
4. Abbreviations including lower case *a* and *b* for left and right side of page.
5. When a single letter is used within a quotation entry, this letter stands for the key word, the first word of the index entry.
6. The importance of the abbreviation "Ibid.", here just Ib.
7. Significance of indention as an indicator of subtopics within the index.

Developing activities:

1. Select words to look up in the concordance that will lead students to quotations they will enjoy. For initial experiences, select a key word having a small number or only one entry. For example, *lipstick* leads to an Ogden Nash couplet from "The Perfect Husband" which says: "He tells you when you've got on too much lipstick, and helps you with your girdle when your hips stick."
2. For more advanced use students could be asked to find out how Benjamin Franklin described himself in his epitaph. They could look up Franklin in the author index, or they could locate Franklin as the subject through the key word in the concordance. Either way, they find he described himself as a printer who had become "food for worms."

*Note: Although there is a 15th edition, published in 1980, the 14th edition was consulted when designing the activities described here.

■ EGYPTIAN HIEROGLYPHS FOR EVERYONE (1968)

Contents of book:

Good textual description of hieroglyphics and their use.

Useful characteristics:

1. Numerous illustrations and line drawings make understanding of glyph symbols relatively simple.
2. Material on the Rosetta Stone is included.
3. There is a dictionary of glyphs and their combinations.

Skills involved:

1. Ability to observe and analyze glyphs.
2. Comprehension of the function of translation.

Developing activities:

1. Find out how the glyphs' meanings were established.
2. Find out how various glyphs are combined for communication.
3. Translate, using the dictionary portion of the book, a short message written in hieroglyphics.
4. Write a message and translate it into Egyptian hieroglyphics.

■ MORRIS DICTIONARY OF WORD AND PHRASE ORIGINS, 3 vols. (1977)

Contents of book:

Paragraph-length entries giving the story behind the creation of words and phrases we use.

Useful characteristics:

1. Multivolumes permit more than one student to work with the dictionary at one time.
2. Alphabetic arrangement from A-Z in each volume.
3. Index provides cross-references.

Skills involved:

1. Alphabetizing.
2. Cross-referencing.
3. Concept that American English words have come from many sources and languages.
4. Concept that language changes as new words and phrases are invented.

Developing activities:

1. Choose entries to be looked up by students for any particular curricular tie-in the teacher wishes to emphasize.
2. Have students choose entries that interest them.
3. Have students choose among entries that begin with an assigned letter.

4. Oral presentations could be made to share findings with the class.
5. The origin could be presented by drawing pictures or by dramatizations.
6. Examples from the dictionary include:
   a. Cole slaw is not "cold slaw." Cole comes from the Latin "colis" which means cabbage, and, slaw, the Dutch word "sla" means salad.
   b. Kid is a pet name for a child since the time of Shakespeare. Really, kid means a young goat, and some people believe that this is the source of the term of endearment. Others point to the German words "kind" meaning child or "kinder" meaning children as the sources of the term kid.

■ ROGET'S THESAURUS OF WORDS AND PHRASES (4th ed., 1977)*

Contents of book:

Thousands of words and phrases arranged according to meaning.

Useful characteristics:

1. Alphabetical index subdivided by meanings or contexts.
2. Antonyms are placed opposite each other on two column pages.
3. Synonyms are grouped according to parts of speech.
4. Paragraphs are numbered.

Skills involved:

1. Alphabetizing.
2. Differentiating between page and paragraph numbers.
3. Recognizing parts of speech.
4. Choosing the most appropriate of the suggested synonyms.
5. Using the index to find the appropriate meaning or concept of the entry word.

Developing activities:

1. Select words that have distinctive multiple meanings or concepts. Initially, chose words that have fewer rather than many concepts. With the word *before,* although the concept of *being in front of* remains the same, there are subtle differences in the

words used in the thesaurus for: *before in order, before in time,* and *before in space.* Students could be asked to find a different word for each of these three meanings.
2. Using the word *leaf,* students could be asked to list synonyms that are nouns, verbs, and adjectives.
3. Give the students a sentence with an overused word, and ask them to replace it with an appropriate synonym, based on the context of the sentence.
4. Once students have become familiar with the use of the thesaurus, a poetry assignment such as writing cinquains would let them apply their skill. A cinquain is a dwarf poem of five lines that follows a strict formula. The first line is one word giving the title. The second line is two words giving a description of the title. The third line is three words expressing an action. The fourth line is four words expressing a feeling. The fifth line is a synonym for the title word.

Example of a cinquain:

Steak
Thick, juicy
Sizzling and spattering
Ready to taste delicious
Meat.

*Note: Copyright date has little effect on the activities described above. There are other editions of Roget such as *Roget's Thesaurus in Dictionary Form,* or junior thesauruses such as *In Other Words II: A Junior Thesaurus.* It is the belief of the authors that differentiated meanings are clearest in the original Roget, and that the simplified versions are useful mainly to introduce the concept of a thesaurus. Their selection of words is so limited that for practical use they are of diminished assistance. Moreover, upper grade elementary student should have no real difficulty using the standard tool.

■ WORLD MYTHOLOGY SERIES, 5 vols. (1983)

Contents of book:

Titles indicate volume content as follows:

Gods, Men and Monsters from Greek Myths
Gods and Heroes from Viking Mythology
Spirits, Heroes and Hunters from North American Indian Mythology
Dragons, Gods and Spirits from Chinese Mythology
Gods and Pharoahs from Egyptian Mythology

Useful characteristics:

1. Table of Contents lists story titles.
2. Index gives characters and key word entries.
3. Each chapter beginning has a box illustrating symbols representative of the nature and adventures of the gods and heroes that follow.
4. There are some colored illustrations and a large number of black and white drawings throughout the set.

Skills involved:

1. Reading comprehension.
2. Ability to use index and table of contents.

Developing activities:

1. Choose a topic or object (brothers or the sun, for example) and compare and contrast its use in the mythology of different cultures.
2. A simpler version of this activity would be simply to find out the character names for the Sun Gods in each of the mythologies.
3. Use a topic such as the role of trickery and find examples of its use in the various mythologies.
4. Analyze a myth of your choice in terms of the standard characteristics of a myth:
   a. An explanation of some natural phenomenon or piece of nature.
   b. Contains characters possessing supernatural strengths.
   c. Some characters are Gods and they interact with human characters.
   d. The events reflect the culture and values of the civilization from which the stories come.

SCIENCE

Science is one of the major segments of the elementary school curriculum. Not only is it important in the classroom, but it lends itself to individual interests and independent studies. Young students are fascinated with experiments, pets, wild animals, space, and many other topics related to science.

Yet, many teachers shy away from science. In most cases they realize that their own backgrounds in science are limited. Also, it takes time to get all the bits and pieces together for a demonstration experiment, and even then it may not succeed. Teachers are understandably uncomfortable with taking the risks involved. While there is no substitute for hands-on science experiments, it is possible to gain valuable experience by using science content while promotiong search skills. Properly designed activities can include basic scientific concepts and hold strong interest for the students.

The library media center's collection provides materials in both the Dewey 500s and 600s—the pure sciences and the applied sciences. The two classifications must be used together to get full coverage of a scientific concept. The applied sciences of medicine or engineering, for example, lead right back to the pure sciences of biology or physics. It is impossible to explore very far while separating the two approaches.

Both general and specific materials are available that cover the many fields of science. Each Dewey subclassification may be expected to have its own specialized history, dictionary, and frequently, encyclopedia. There will be, for example, manuals for the identification of individual species of plants, animals, and minerals such as the popular ones by Zim. Because one needs simpler material for elementary reference, many trade books will need to be used. These may not be considered reference books in the usual sense, but the science section in the school library media center needs to be generously possessed of reference materials on a wide variety of levels.

Young children are inclined to be avid collectors. Although such interests may be classed as hobbies rather than formal curriculumn-related learning, many of the same materials will be used for both purposes. For this reason the majority of the science collection titles need not be placed in a true reference section. In addition, the very easiest natural history materials will receive extensive use if they are placed along with fiction in a section classified as "Easy." Although there is definite curricular use to be made of these materials, equally important is the recreational use made of them.

The rapidity with which technology, and science in general, has been moving forward means that there are constantly new considerations and developments to address in collection building. The children will come looking for materials on any new topic, sometimes before anything is available for them in book form. Therefore, the school library media teacher should be alert to the new topic terminologies and guide students toward their use. The younger students will not be aware of terms such as *Alzheimer's disease, AIDS, Compact discs,* or *Starwars (Strategic Defense Initiative)* being newly added. They will have those terms in their vocabularies from the start. However, numerous geographic name changes such as Kampuchea for Cambodia or Sri Lanka for Ceylon, or developing terms such as *Interactive fiction* or *Twenty-first century* that have been incorporated under other terminology until becoming established independently as subject headings, will cause students indexing problems. They will need help in getting these relationships together when they are doing retrospective searching.

One hears discussion among school library media teachers regarding another terminology situation, one that probably troubles the teachers more than it does the students. Nonetheless, it calls for teacher awareness if students are to receive needed instruction.

As smaller community and school libraries join networks, as databases become increasingly available for student use, and as printed catalog cards offer Sears' subject headings less frequently, school library media teachers note the prevalence of Library of Congress Subject Headings terminology. The vocabulary of LCSH may need to be pointed out to students using these sources, but once identified these terms are just as easy as others to learn to look up. It is difficult to justify maintaining different terminology in elementary school library media center indexing when the whole point is for students to develop skills which equip and encourage them to use other libraries.

■ GROLIER'S AMAZING WORLD OF ANIMALS, 20 vols. (1972)

Contents of book:

Good coverage of the animal kingdom. Includes lesser known animals for which information is often difficult to locate. In index volume there is a section on endangered species arranged by continents. Good colored pictures and line drawings to show details.

Useful characteristics:

1. Each volume contains a table of contents and an index.
2. There is a cumulative index volume.
3. Topics are clearly subdivided and headings are obvious.
4. Some maps are included.

Skills involved:

1. Alphabetizing.
2. Skimming.
3. Reading for content.

Developing activities:

1. Choose interesting terms in the index and check them out. For example, *ghost limpet* is listed. Why the name "ghost" limpet? (Shell markings suggest the impression of a human hand.)
   In another example, *Tasmanian devil* has multiple listings to be found in two different volumes, four articles are in one volume, and one is in the other. Students might be asked to find a picture of a Tasmanian devil, find out how long it lives, the category of animals to which it belongs (marsupial), and explain what it and an opposum have in common.

■ **LET'S DISCOVER, 16 vols. (1980)**

Contents of book:

Mostly scientific topics presented in simple, straightforward text. Well illustrated. Some social life and customs included.

Divided into volumes thematically as their titles indicate:

Prehistoric World
Cold Blooded Animals
Warm Blooded Animals
The Earth
The Sea
You and Your Body
The World of Machines
Land and Travels
Ships and Boats
Flying
Outer Space
Sport and Entertainment
People and Customs
People of Long Ago
What People Do

Useful characteristics:

1. Final cumulative index volume.
2. Individual volumes contain index, glossary, bibliography, questions to think about, and suggested projects.
3. Print is larger than usual size and is easily read.
4. Boxed information visually highlights certain facts, making it easier to compare and contrast features of the topic; e.g., beaks and hoofs for animals, weapons for early man, and sails on ships. Sometimes the boxed information explains a process such as how airplane ejection seats work, or diagrams the interior of a 747 plane.

Skills involved:

1. Alphabetizing.
2. Use of boxes and picture captions.
3. Reading for content.

Developing activities:

1. Start with the indexes; examine picture captions and boxes. An adaptation of *Trivial Pursuit* was prepared for an evening

program at sixth grade Outdoor Education camp. Using the volumes that fitted the outdoor curriculum (i.e., those on animals, the earth, its weather), questions such as the following were devised:

a. What do you call a tree that loses its leaves? (Deciduous.)
b. What do all conifers produce? (Cones to house their seeds.)
c. What is the name of white, fluffy clouds? (Cumulus.)
d. How many toes does a cloven hoofed animal have? (Two.)
e. What is the name of the animal whose parents are a zebra and a donkey? (Zedonk.)

■ LIVING EARTH, 20 vols. (1973)

Contents of book:

The science of ecology, food chains, and predator/prey relationships are addressed in the beginning of the last volume. Additionally, titles of volumes indicate areas of emphasis as follows:

Desert Life
Forest Life
Natural Man
Every Living Thing
Invisible World
Earth's Crust
Air Around Us
World of Plants
Grassland Life
Seas and Oceans
Rivers and Lakes
Mountain Life
Polar Life
Island Life
Nature in the City
Web of Life
Pollution
Conservation
Life in the Future
Guide and Index

Useful characteristics:

1. Colored photographs.
2. Excellent diagrams.
3. Index in each volume.
4. Cumulative index and guide in last volume.

Skills involved:

1. Use of volume codes in cumulative index.
2. Skimming.
3. Note taking.
4. Interpretation of diagrams and charts.

Developing activities:

1. Fact finding can be tied to the concepts being studied, or can be based on picture captions and charts. Because there are few subheadings in the text, and because the text is extensive, the reference is more suitable for advanced students working on a long term project.
2. Younger students could gain information from the pictures and make generalizations about regions of the earth.

■ RAINTREE ILLUSTRATED SCIENCE ENCYCLOPEDIA, 20 vols. (1978)

Contents of book:

Short entries on scientific subjects are arranged alphabetically. Adequately illustrated with charts and pictures, but more print and fewer pictures than some other similar references. Two projects are outlined at the end of each volume and are keyed to its content.

Useful characteristics:

1. Half of the final volume is an index to the set.
2. A bibliography arranged by subject precedes the index.
3. Each volume has a page on the use of the encyclopedia, cross-references, and pronunciation.
4. Articles are signed.

Skills involved:

1. Alphabetizing.
2. Use of cross-references.
3. Reading for content.

Developing activities:

1. Examine the index for interesting topics, then check them out in the appropriate volume. Questions to pose: a. What is the

purpose of a *microtome?* (To slice thin sections embedded in wax for viewing under a microscope.) b. What is the name of a baby eel? (Elver.) c. What happens to you when you walk through a patch of nettles? (Legs sting and itch.) d. List and define types of mining. (Methods of Mining paragraph lists eight.)

■ SCIENCE AND TECHNOLOGY ILLUSTRATED, 28 vols. (1984)

Contents of book:

Topics related to natural science and applications of technological invention through the twentieth century.

Useful characteristics:

1. Colorful illustrations.
2. Graphic representations of complex concepts.
3. Subheadings.
4. Some maps.
5. Table of Contents in each volume.
6. Cumulative index for set is in last volume.

Skills involved:

1. Alphabetizing.
2. Use of cross references.
3. Reading for content.

Developing activities:

Select topics from the index or tables of contents that relate to ongoing classroom activity and develop questions requiring the location of specific information. For example, find out about the resurgence of interest in wind power; or find out how wind helps or hinders people.

Fine Arts

Music, art, speech, and drama may be approached as an integral part of the curriculum, or they may be pursued in separate classes with specialist teachers. When they are a part of the regular curriculum, art and music are often integrated with social studies as part of the record of a country's achievements. Also, the texts of songs, plays, and operas may be related to language arts. The degree of emphasis placed on the arts will vary widely among school systems. However, programs for the gifted, independent study projects, and children's personal interests will place demands on this part of the collection even if the curriculum does not.

■ CATHEDRAL (1973)

Contents of book:

The construction of a cathedral by the people of Chutreaux, over a period of eighty-six years (1252-1338), is described in detail. Black and white line drawings illustrate clearly the intricate steps of construction from the initial planning to the dedication ceremonies. The contributions of each of the building crafts involved are made clear.

Useful characteristics:

1. The detail of the drawings verifies the adage concerning the worth of pictures.
2. A glossary appears at the end.
3. The arrangement is chronological, and follows the construction steps.

Skills involved:

1. Ability to read.
2. Ability to observe and learn from drawings.

Developing activities:

1. Basic architectural terms are valuable additions to vocabulary. Use the terms in the glossary identifying their architectural purpose in the structure of a cathedral.
2. If there is a large church or a cathedral in your area, visit it and see how many of these architectural devices are present in it.
3. The author has created other books such as *Castle, City, Pyramid,* and *Underground.* They may be used in similar fashion. The following activities could be carried out using *Castle:*
   a. Study the basic architectural terms that are found in the glossary. Study their structural details and their underlying purposes and use them to gain an understanding of life and living conditions. For example, the *batter* is a slanted base extending out from a vertical wall. When stones were dropped from the wall above (during a battle), the slant caused the stones to ricochet and injure or kill attacking soldiers. Additionally, the batter reinforced the walls.
   b. Discuss the importance of having a well located within the castle itself.
   c. Discuss the methods of defense in terms of architectural structure.
   d. Discuss the methods of attack in terms of architectural structure.

■ ROOFS OVER AMERICA (1967)

Contents of book:

The architectural feature that is probably the simplest to recognize—the roof—is the focus of this book. Black and white photographs and effective text on adjacent pages trace architectural styles from the colonial period through the 1960s.

Useful characteristics:

1. The brief text includes the social and economic reasons for the changes in style.
2. Chronological arrangement is used.

Skills involved:

1. Ability to read.
2. Ability to observe.

Developing activities:

1. Depending on the age of the students, group discussion or individual search could be centered on questions such as the following:
   a. Describe the adaptation of a Cape Cod cottage into a "salt box" house. Find out (using an additional source) the relationship of salt box houses to the taxation scheme of the time. Compare this taxation system with that applied to the mansard roof in Paris.
   b. What were the advantages of the gambrel roof design?
   c. What does *Georgian* mean? What were the essential characteristics of a Georgian building? What is a "widow's walk" and what purpose does it serve?
   d. Describe some recent developments in roof styles and identify the advantages of each.
2. Take photographs of buildings in your own area that have examples of the types of roofs described in the book. Find out, if you can, when each of these buildings was constructed.
3. Take additional photographs of the newest buildings in your area. Do they repeat the past or demonstrate new ideas?
4. Make a display of the photographs for the school.

■ WORLD ATLAS OF ARCHITECTURE (1984)

Contents of book:

Major sections of the book address non-European civilizations, the Ancient world, late antiquity and the early Middle Ages, the Middle Ages, the age of Classicism, and the modern era. Each is subdivided by geographic locations or chronology.

Useful characteristics:

1. Detailed four color maps show the great empires and the location of important archaeological sites and architectural masterpieces.
2. Timeline charts integrate key events in history with the construction of monuments.

3. Unusual perspective and cut-away drawings are accompanied by brief text and illustrate structural features of buildings.
4. Hundreds of color photographs are included.
5. The index and glossary are combined.

Skills involved:

1. Index skills.
2. Skimming.
3. Interpretation of drawings and charts.
4. Map reading.

Developing activities:

1. Looking at the timeline chart of civilization and architecture for China, what was built in and near Peking during the Ming Dynasty?
2. List the different building materials used in Africa to construct houses.
3. Give two reasons why there are few surviving examples of Egyptian domestic architecture.
4. Name at least one French, English, and Spanish gothic cathedral.
5. What was the most popular building of the Paris Exhibition of 1889? List the criteria for building an exposition hall in the 1800s.

■ YOUNG PERSON'S GUIDE TO BALLET (1975)

Contents of book:

The author yearned to see and study dancing as a young girl. Only later was this possible. She has written the book to help children grasp something of the training of a dancer, the history of dance, and, most especially, to realize that, "quite apart from a career, dancing is a lovely thing to be able to do and, because you have learnt something about it, watching dancing will give you pleasure all your life."

Useful characteristics:

1. Material is presented skillfully.
2. Diagrams of steps and photos of leading dancers are included.
3. Emphasis is placed on the changing attitude toward male dancers.

4. Although there is no index, technical terms and titles (printed in italics) stand out in the text.

Skills involved:

1. Ability to read with understanding.
2. Ability to interpret diagrams.

Developing activities:

1. Read the book and look for answers to questions such as the following:
   a. Name the five basic ballet steps and describe them.
   b. Find out about the history of ballet. Who is responsible for the start of ballet in the USSR?
   c. Describe a young dance student's instructional routine. In what field do you believe you could work hard enough to become successful?
   d. What is mime and what is its role in ballet?
   e. Choose one famous ballet and tell its story.
   f. Choose one well-known ballet dancer and find out about that person's life.
   g. What has been America's contribution to ballet?
2. Arrange to see a ballet performance.

■ DISCOVERING ART HISTORY (1981)

Contents of book:

Emphasis is on European and American art with a brief overview of art from the non-Western world. The text is arranged chronologically from prehistoric times to the present. Initial chapters address materials used by artists and design concepts.

Useful characteristics:

1. Pronunciation guides for artists' names, places and terms.
2. Includes a glossary, a bibliography, and an index.
3. Small, mostly black-and-white, photographs are interspersed throughout the text.

Skills involved:

1. Alphabetic order in index.
2. Skimming for information.
3. Use of boldface subheadings to locate passages.

Developing activities:

1. Use index or browse through the book to devise questions that will further the purpose of the assignment. Some questions might be for class discussion; others for individual answering.
   a. Compare the development of Etruscan art with the development of Greek art.
   b. What was El Greco's real name and when did he live?
   c. How was William Hogarth's fame established? When and where did he live?
   d. What strongly influenced James Whistler? What colors did he use mostly?
   e. What museums do you find pictures of in this book? Are any of them near where you live?
2. If the school has a print collection, a gallery show could be selected by the students. Base the show on a theme or time period. Have students prepare information about each print writing on only one side of a card that can be posted next to the picture when it is hung.
3. Visit a local art show and have students look for paintings that have characteristics they have learned about.

■ LOOKING AT ART: PEOPLE AT HOME (1982)

Contents of book:

Thirty-five color reproductions of famous paintings. Artists are representative of various countries and periods of time. All paintings are associated with the theme *People at Home*. (Other themes in the series include *Faces* and *People at Work*).

Useful characteristics:

1. Text explains the picture and directs attention to interesting points that might otherwise be overlooked.
2. Pictures tend to be "paired" to provide comparing and contrasting opportunities.
3. Social life and conditions expressed in the paintings are pointed out in the text.
4. Brief biographical sketches of the painters are included.
5. Both an index and a table of contents are provided.

Skills involved:

1. Ability to read.
2. Ability to observe.

Developing activities:

1. If insufficient copies of the book are available for use as a text, reproductions could be projected on an opaque projector. If the projection method is used, the teacher could use the text as a guide for group discussion of the paintings and their messages.
2. If used as a text, students could be asked to answer questions such as the following:
   a. Of what historical use are works of art?
   b. Use examples under the chapter heading "Couples." What similarities and what differences can you find between the couples of 1743 and 1970?
   c. What part does the window play in the pictures by Hopper and Tissot in the "Cold Shoulder" chapter?
   d. In the "Reading for Pleasure" chapter paintings, what clues suggest the readers are enjoying themselves?
   e. What does the use of the curved (rather than a standard flat) mirror enable the artist to do with the reflections? How does this influence the paintings?
   f. Speculate on reasons Picasso painted his version of *Las Meninas* when Velasquez had already used the same subject.
   g. Contrast family life as shown by Pippin's *The Dominoe Players* and Matisse's *The Painter's Family*.
   h. Can one always depend upon the "facts" found in a painting? Consider *The Saltonstall Family* when giving your answer.

■ PAINTINGS: HOW TO LOOK AT GREAT ART (n.d.)

Contents of book:

Using examples from prehistoric cave paintings to Cezanne, the author explains the meaning of such concepts as design, pattern, composition, space, perspective, light and shade, and movement. Emphasis is on teaching your eyes to see things in a painting which will lead you to see more in your everyday world.

Useful characteristics:

1. Most reproductions of the paintings being used as examples are in color.
2. A timeline of major events in world history is paired with the works of art described.
3. A small biographical dictionary of the artists whose works are discussed is provided.
4. An index is included.

Skills involved:

1. Use of index and table of contents.
2. Skimming for information.

Developing activities:

1. In the picture *St. George and the Dragon* by Paolo Uccello, how does the artist keep drawing your eye to the dragon's mouth?
2. Look at Jan Van Eyck's picture *Portrait of Giovanni Arnolfini and His Wife*. List the different textures you could feel that are illustrated in this picture.
3. When looking at Pieter Bruegel the Elder's *The Peasant Wedding,* what sounds do you almost hear?
4. List the similarities and differences between Winslow Homer's *Long Branch, New Jersey* and your day at the beach.
5. How did Claude Monet give the impression of sunlight in his picture titled *Water Lilies, Midday?*

■ STORY OF AMERICAN ART FOR YOUNG PEOPLE (1978)

Contents of book:

Begins with the art of the American Indian and the simple creations of the European settlers and continues with sections devoted to the eighteenth century, the American Revolution, the nineteenth century, and the twentieth century. Emphasis is on major movements and individual artists of each period.

Useful charactristics:

1. Includes sixty-five color reproductions and about one hundred black-and-white photographs.
2. Chapter topics correlate well with social studies units in American history.

Skills involved:

1. Use of table of contents.
2. Skimming for information.
3. Ability to appreciate and interpret the illustrations.

Developing activities:

Questions that are devised may match the social studies unit being studied or they may center on the artistic aspects of the art works. Sample questions follow:
a. How were porcupine quills used by the Eastern Woodland Indians?
b. What kind of paintings did the English settlers have? Why?
c. What was unusual about Benjamin West's painting *The Death of Wolfe?* What two things did West do for the first time?
d. How did the ideas of the Nineteenth-century romantics differ from the early settlers' ideas about art?
e. Cassat, an American impressionist, was particularly good at painting what? What didn't she paint?

■ HOME BOOK OF MUSICAL KNOWLEDGE (1954)

Contents of book:

The book is divided into seven parts:

The A.B.C. of music, its history and composers
Choral and vocal music
Music for the stage: the opera and the ballet
Music for solo instruments and for chamber music groups
Orchestral music
Music for children
Glossary of basic terms in music.

Useful characteristics:

1. Brief biographies of composers.
2. Synopses of stories used in ballets and operas.
3. Descriptions of the meaning of selected orchestral works.
4. Extensive index.

Skills involved:

1. Index skills
2. Skimming skills.
3. Alphabetic order for locating entries within sections.

Developing activities:

1. At what age did Mahler show an interest in music? What did he do in addition to composing music?
2. What is the definition of a *serenade* as a vocal form of music?
3. Which composer is mentioned the most times in the list of one hundred basic orchestral works?
4. What is the plot of the opera *Peter Grimes?*
5. Britten wrote a piece of music to introduce children to the instruments of the orchestra. What is it called? What other piece of music with the same purpose is mentioned in this section?

■ MUSIC DICTIONARY (1956)

Contents of book:

Over eight hundred concise definitions of musical terms interspersed with drawings to explain the text.

Useful characteristics:

1. Use of simple language and practical illustrations to help the young music student understand the concepts most likely to be encountered.
2. Phonetic pronunciations are included as are a list of musical abbreviations and signs.

Skills involved:

1. Alphabetical order.
2. Pronunciation symbols.
3. No guide words are used.

Developing activities:

Select specific terms for the students to look up such as the following:
   a. How does a *reed* produce a musical sound?
   b. What does a *dot* do to the length of a note?
   c. When was *Baroque* music written?
   d. What do you do if your part is marked *tacet?*
   e. What term do you have to look under to find the definition of a *gong?*

■ WHAT INSTRUMENT SHALL I PLAY? (1976)

Contents of book:

Text addresses how sounds are made, why instruments produce different sounds, how instruments work, and sections on instruments grouped traditionally as: strings, woodwinds, brasses, percussion, keyboard instruments, and non-orchestral instruments.

Useful characteristics:

1. Photographs and line drawings illustrate the text.
2. Includes nonorchestral instruments that are often difficult to find; for example, the tin whistle made prominent by flutist James Gallway, the harmonica, or the bagpipes. A synthesizer is included among keyboard instruments.
3. Glossary.
4. Both table of contents and index.

Skills involved:

1. Alphabetizing.
2. Associating picture captions with correct picture.
3. Skimming. (Articles are short but without subheads.)

Developing activities:

1. If you already play an instrument, read about it, and list five interesting facts about its history or playing.
2. Choose one instrument from each of the divisions (Chapters 5 through 33) and find a characteristic that would encourage you to learn to play that instrument.
3. How is sound made for each category of instrument?
4. In what types of instrumental groups are these instruments played?
5. Explain how reeds, strings, or valves are made and cared for.
6. If students in the class or in the school play these instruments, organize a demonstration "party" for other students to hear and see these instruments.
7. Plan to attend a concert together.

■ WHO'S WHO IN ROCK (1981)

Contents of book:

Contains paragraph length biographies of twelve hundred personalities involved with rock and roll and popular music. Emphasis is placed on how a person or group fits into the overall scheme of rock, what they are famous or best remembered for, and their effect on popular music.

Useful characteristics:

1. Arranged in dictionary style with boldface headings.
2. Numerous photographs add to the book's usefulness.
3. Detailed index.

Skills involved:

1. Alphabetizing.
2. Skimming for facts.

Developing activities:

Use the index or leaf through the book to devise questions suitable for the purpose of the assignment. Questions could resemble the following examples:
    a. Browse through the entries and list three of the oddest names for a performing group that you can find.
    b. What aspect of the Everly Brothers' style most influenced the history of popular music?
    c. Chuck Berry was in trouble with the law three times. What did he do each time and what were the consequences?
    d. Who did Professor Longhair influence? What instrument did he play?
    e. What was the original name for Sonny and Cher when they first struck out on their own?

■ ROOSTER'S HORNS (1978)

Contents of book:

Chinese folk tale prepared for presentation as shadow puppet play or as a simple story to be read. You will never hear a rooster crow again without remembering this tale!

Useful characteristics:

1. Text written so that it easily becomes the lines for performance. In addition, suggested beginnings to the play are provided.
2. Patterns for making the characters (only two—plus a finger), and clear and simple directions for the technical aspects of the production are included.
3. Contains the listing of the animals for the twelve year cycle.

Skills involved:

1. Following directions.
2. Memorizing lines.

Developing activities:

1. Read the story emphasizing the flattery and the psychological overtones.
2. Produce the play.
   a. Select four voice participants—three characters plus a narrator to introduce and close the play.
   b. Select students to make the puppets. Photocopy patterns in the book to use to cut and trace.
   c. Select students to manipulate the puppets, the sun, and the worm.
   d. Select students to collect and set up "stage" equipment.
   e. Practice responsibilities individually. Then practice them as a group to learn how to coordinate movements without interfering with other manipulators.
   f. Present the shadow puppet play for another class, parents, or in a home for the elderly.
3. Write original plays or adapt other familiar stories or legends into shadow puppet plays.

■ ENCYCLOPEDIA OF TOYS (1978)

Contents of book:

Information is given about the following categories of toys: miniature living, toys purely for pleasure, wheeled toys and children's transport, metal toys, board and table games, educational toys, and pastimes. Historical background is given describing how each toy has changed over time. Attention is given to toys of the eighteenth, nineteenth, and twentieth centuries in both the United States and abroad.

Useful characteristics:

1. Includes over three hundred black-and-white illustrations and seventy color pictures.
2. Original advertisements are included in the illustrations.
3. There is a comprehensive index.
4. Advice is given about the care and cleaning of old toys.
5. An alphabetical list of manufactures is provided.

Skills involved:

1. Use of an index and table of contents.
2. Matching captions to the correct illustrations by interpreting directions such as *right, below right, bottom,* etc.
3. Skimming for a fact.

Developing activities:

1. What types of toys are included in the section "Toys Purely for Pleasure?"
2. On what pages will you find information about board games?
3. What is the story about the original teddy bear? What have teddy bears been made of?
4. How many different manufacturers of child-sized cars are mentioned?
5. What was Milton Bradley's first published board game? When was his business established and how did he choose to manufacture games?

Social Studies and History

The social studies are the part of the curriculum that provides an understanding of people and their cultures. In the primary grades the areas learned about are the home, school, and community life in the United States. Successive grades include such topics as citizenship, social life and customs, life styles, communications, transportation, food, shelter, protection, careers, etc. Comparisons are made between life in the United States and in other countries of the world.

In the upper grades, history takes on even greater importance. Units frequently include the antiquities of Greece and Rome, the Middle Ages, the age of exploration, and the development of the United States. Some attention is given to Native Americans, and to immigration and various ethnic groups.

Few areas of the school library media center's collection contain a wider range of materials, or offer more opportunity to develop search activities suitable for augmenting classroom activity. A wide variety of experiences can be devised based on the use of such materials as chronologies, geographical references, pictorial histories, social histories, or civil histories of the world or an individual country or state.

Chronologies

A chronology is a timesaving tool. It will not satisfy all needs, and additional information will have to be obtained elsewhere; but it is a splendid beginning. Whenever an assignment deals with people and the times in which they lived, and the objective includes finding what events and what people were contemporary with each other, there is no better tool.

Most chronologies mix people and events. Some of them use topical headings to help differentiate and categorize people and events. An example of this approach is found in the three volume set, *Chronology of the Ancient World, Chronology of the Expanding World,* and *Chronology of the Modern World* in which a two-page spread is devoted to a given year. The topical headings guide one to useful references.

Other chronologies divide pages into columns and assign topical headings to the columns. Dates are listed in the page margin. An example of this arrangement is found in *Timetables of History.* Langer's *Encyclopedia of World History* provides considerable amounts of text. The table of contents is arranged chronologically and geographically to help readers find material. A detailed index is available for when a specific name or event is known.

The chronology which would find the most use in elementary school is *Who Was When? A Dictionary of Contemporaries.* The listings are limited to people's birth and death dates placed in columns under the discipline to which they contributed. An alphabetic index also provides the person's dates, and the user is led to the proper page by knowing the birth date.

When one understands the correlation between the information given in the chronology (name, date-span, and profession) and the arrangement of collected biography (date-span, profession, and geographic area), it becomes fairly easy to find the additional information needed to complete a report.

Another instance in which a chronology proves its worth is when there is need to construct a timeline. In this case a chronology arranged by topical headings proves most useful.

■ **WHO WAS WHEN?** *A Dictionary of Contemporaries (3rd ed., 1976)*

Contents of book:

Identifies contemporaries in various professions from 500 B.C. to A.D. 1974. Provides only the year of birth and death, except in the case of popes and monarchs. Here the dates given refer to assuming and relinquishing the title rather than actual birth and death dates.

Useful characteristics:

1. Arranged chronologically with guide dates on each page.
2. Information is listed in columns.
3. Dates run top-to-bottom in the margins.
4. Eleven fields of accomplishment are spread across the page.
5. Abbreviations are used with each person's name to indicate what happened in that year.

Skills involved:

1. Chronological sequence.
2. Alphabetizing.
3. Categorizing.
4. Using guide dates at top of page to identify the range covered on a two-page spread.
5. Using abbreviations and the key to explain unfamiliar ones located in the front of the reference book.
6. Learning to consult the pages that precede and follow exact dates in order to include the widest range of comtemporaries.
7. Becoming able to learn about the person's contributions by using encyclopedias and biographical references.

Developing activities:

1. Assign an individual to each student and have them search for the following information:

a. Look in the alphabetical index to find the birth and death dates of the assigned individual.
   b. Locate appropriate pages that list that person and his or her contemporaries.
   c. For initial experiences, students could be asked to name someone born the same year and someone who died the same year as the assigned individual.
   d. At the next level, students could be asked to identify contemporaries from specific categories such as government, science, or the arts. Categories labeled "Literature," "Painting & Sculpture," and "Music" go together to make up the one termed "Arts."
2. When this tool is used increasingly and at a more sophisticated level, the library media teacher will need to provide more guidance in selecting names of contemporaries to study further. Otherwise, names chosen may not appear in materials within the collection. For example, students who have read a piece of historical fiction may be asked as part of their reports on this reading to identify three individuals living at the time represented in the book. Students would then identify where these persons lived and what they did.
3. Given a list of names related to a period of history, the students could create a chart showing the overlapping of their life spans, whether during the period of the ancient Greeks, the American Revolution, Civil War period, or other period.

Geographical References

Study of the regions of the earth and geography is a major component of most elementary school curricula. Geography is also a by-product of the study of other nations, cultures, and economics. Of necessity, geographical references play an important role in the elementary school library media center collection. Happily, there are increasing numbers of atlases, gazetteers, and other books of geographic orientation appearing for the youngest students. It is with them that the initial introduction to using maps takes place, often by mapping the classroom or locating one's home on a simple community map.

History is seldom taught without reference to maps and globes. Science study employs moon globes and topographical maps. Specialized or thematic atlases are prepared for showing the homelands of animals, butterflies, or plants and trees of the world. In these and other specialized atlases there is a trend toward including colorful illustrations and a significant amount of text which turns them into more of a reference book than a traditional maps-only style of atlas.

Regardless of the type of atlas, the student must learn to use grid codes for locating references found in the atlas index, recognize directions, interpret symbols, and eventually comprehend scale. Recognition of the difference between historical and modern maps is required.

The term *gazetteer* applies both to the alphabetic index of the atlas when it includes some statistics, or to a single volume reference book. The single volume reference book includes almost no maps. Instead, the geographic information is arranged alphabetically and indicates whether a given term stands for a city, county, river, mountain, or other geographical feature. Usually some historical and descriptive text is added, it varies in length from a single line to several paragraphs. Especially useful is a gazetteer with the title of a dictionary, for example, *Webster's New Geographical Dictionary.*

Travel guides provide additional detailed information about the various states or foreign countries. Automobile associations, Fodor, Michelin, and others produce useful travel publications.

Specialized books such as the *Standard Encyclopedia of the World's Mountains, Oceans and Islands,* and *Rivers and Lakes* (three separate volumes) are quite usable for elementary school students.

Sets such as *Lands and Peoples* or the *Worldmark Encyclopedia of Nations* provide comprehensive geographic information and more.

There are numerous series or sets based on the individual states of the United States and on countries around the world. Useful among these are Carpenter's *Enchantment of America,* or Fradin's *In Words and Pictures* series for states; and the *Macdonald Countries, Let's Travel In . . ., Looking at Other Countries, My Village In . . .,* or *Life In Other Lands* series for countries of the world.

Attention should be called to the publication *Maps on File.* These current maps are produced to facilitate the easy making of duplication masters and transparencies. Although the expense might prohibit purchase of this excellent reference tool by some small schools, surely most school systems could subscribe to the service and devise a method whereby all schools in the district could share in its use. No atlas matches *Maps on File* for currency or range and variety of content.

■ RAND McNALLY HISTORICAL ATLAS OF THE WORLD (1975, paper)

Contents of book:

Worldwide, primarily political maps from A.D. 200 to 1961.

Useful characteristics:

1. Fairly simple, uncluttered, color maps.
2. Arranged by date and subdivided into geographic areas.

3. Table of contents shows that in order to trace the complete history of a geographic region, several sections of the book must be consulted.
4. Index provides grid markings as well as pages.

Skills involved:

1. Alphabetizing.
2. Map reading, grid locations.
3. Interpreting symbols in map key.
4. Recognizing the difference between modern and historical maps.

Developing activities:

Select a map that represents a time period and geographic area being studied. Scan the map to find relationships to concepts and events being studied in the classroom. For example, the map of the Roman Empire, about A.D. 400 might generate questions of this sort:
   a. Using companion modern maps, list present day countries that were included in each of the Roman Prefectures of Gaul, Italy, Illyricum, and The East.
   b. Determine which group of barbarians made the longest journeys.

■ NATIONAL GEOGRAPHIC PICTURE ATLAS OF OUR FIFTY STATES (1980)

Contents of book:

Four-page entries for each state highlighting important facts related to that state. Includes a product map, state symbols, and colored pictures representative of the area. There are also regional write-ups and special features such as weather and climate, agriculture, and energy. Includes the District of Columbia and outlying territories.

Useful characteristics:

1. Indexed.
2. Presentation of states grouped by standard geographic regions.

Skills involved:

1. Map reading.
2. Skimming skills.

Developing activities:

1. Choose a region and create a map question and a couple of skimming questions for each state in the region.
2. When developing map questions, try to vary the type of information asked for or the skill to be used. For example: a. Peoria is what direction from Springfield? b. What does the yellow mean on the Wisconsin map? (Indian Reservation) c. Two rivers in Iowa are named for animals. What are they? d. Name the town at the intersection of Routes 10 and 71. e. What two roads meet in the town of Rolla? f. How tall are the Glass Mountains?
3. Use a key word from the text within the question to allow the student to skim for that word. Students need to be taught to determine the key word in a question and to use it to avoid reading the entire passage word for word. Once the key word has been found, the student will need to read the sentence or paragraph carefully to find the information requested. When designing skimming questions don't overlook information in picture captions. The following questions might be used: a. During what years did Johnny Appleseed tramp across central Ohio? This question requires the student to look for dates within the text. b. In what Iowa city is the nation's largest popcorn plant located? The key word here is *popcorn*.

■ NATIONAL GEOGRAPHIC PICTURE ATLAS OF OUR WORLD (1980)

Contents of book:

Maps of continents and of countries on each continent are accompanied by text, basic facts, flags, and colored pictures of the localities. Maps give physical features, principal cities, products, and transportation routes.

Useful characteristics:

1. Indexed.
2. Maps are uncluttered.

3. Maps are supplied with grid indicators.
4. Island nations are well presented.
5. Unfamiliar words are explained.
6. List of superlatives is included: deepest, longest, highest, etc.
7. Special feature articles on mapping, geological forces, habitats, population, etc.

Skills involved:

1. Alphabetizing.
2. Reading and interpreting map symbols.
3. Reading and interpreting a map grid.
4. Skimming.

Developing activities:

1. Map study and skimming practice are the two major uses of the book.
2. Using the entry on Mexico, a map study question could call for the identification of the two peninsulas that extend from the mainland. A bit more difficult challenge would be to identify the bodies of water separated by each of these peninsulas. In the one instance this information is given on the map. In the other instance, the information is found in the final paragraph of the textual entry.
2. For skimming questions on Mexico one could ask, "What is carried in rebozos?" (a child); or "What are causes for fiestas?" (soccer game, rodeo, religious holiday, independence day).
4. Using the entry for Japan, map skills practice might involve having students identify the island on which Mt. Fuji is located, or locating cities that have international airports.
5. A skimming activity for Japan could call for the identification of *sushi*, or identifying the job of a *people pusher*.

■ LANDS AND PEOPLES, 6 vols. (1981)

Contents of book:

The title is descriptive. The scope is worldwide. The volumes are allocated two to Europe and one each to Africa, Central and South America, North America, and Island nations. Colored photographs and maps are used as illustrations.

Useful characteristics:

1. Subheadings are good.
2. Flags of the nations are included.
3. A "fact box" is given at the start of each country's entry, and includes information on life style and cultural and ethnic customs.
4. Indexed.
5. Includes lists of assorted facts such as superlatives, major languages, chronology of world history, geographic terms, metric conversion tables, etc.
6. Economic, climate, and time zone maps included.

Skills involved:

1. Alphabetizing.
2. Fact finding.
3. Reading for content.
4. Using subheadings.

Developing activities:

1. Traditional basic information about peoples and the lands they live in is provided. Comparisons among countries are eased by the commonality of subject subheadings used throughout the reference volumes.
2. Sample questions on Iraq follow:
   a. What is the old name for Iraq? (Mesopotamia.)
   b. Who are the Kurds? Why do problems exist between them and the Iraqi government? (They are not Arabs.)
   c. The Kurds are *nomadic*. What does this mean? (No fixed residence.)
   d. Describe the interior of a nomad's tent. (Picture shows use of rugs and equipment.)
   e. How hot do the desert areas get? (120 degrees F.)
3. Sample questions on Nigeria follow:
   a. What is the language generally used? (English.)
   b. How many local languages are spoken? (250.)
   c. Do you have difficulty understanding someone from another part of the U.S.? If so, what do we call this difference in speech sounds? (Dialect.)
   d. What is the effect of dialects for the Ibo people? (It is difficult to understand each other.)

4. Sample questions on Australia follow:
   a. What is unique about the Australian people? (They have a whole continent to themselves.)
   b. How long is the coastline? (12,000 miles.)
   c. What is the unusual characteristic of Australia's mountains and why? (They are the flattest in the world because of their age.)
   d. What effect does being in the southern hemisphere have on Christmas in Australia? (It is celebrated with a picnic at the beach.)
   e. What tree is on their coat of arms? (Acacia.) What is its other name and how did the tree get it? (Wattle, because the branches are especially good for wattle and daub construction used by the settlers.)

■ WEBSTER'S NEW GEOGRAPHICAL DICTIONARY (1980)

Contents of book:

Alphabetic arrangement of geographical information is given in short entry form with only a few maps.

Useful characteristics:

1. Explanatory notes on use of book.
2. Abbreviations and symbols chart.
3. Geographic terms given in English and in foreign languages for ease of comparison and identification.
4. Map symbols chart.
5. Map projections article and illustrations on endpapers.
6. History of geographic location given in write-up.

Skills involved:

1. Alphabetic arrangement for finding entries.
2. Ability to use abbreviations.
3. Ability to understand symbols.
4. Multiple meanings are given within entries so the user must be able to recognize where one stops and the next starts, and that there are multiple uses of a term.
5. Comprehension of latitude and longitude, of elevation and depth, and of length and direction.

Developing activities:

The questions devised must tie in with the studies of the moment. Samples of types of questions that could be used follow:
- a. Use your assigned letter of the alphabet and choose a geographic name that appeals to you. Tell what it is; i.e., city, mountain, river, etc., and where it is. What additional information is provided?
- b. Find your chosen term on an atlas map, if possible.
- c. For how many different geographical features is the name *Hudson* used?
- d. You are writing a story and are setting it in an imaginary country you call *Istokpoga*. Check to see if this is a real name and if you should change your chosen name to make it fictional.
- e. What is meant by map *projection?* Why are there different projections in use?
- f. By what other names is Mt. Fuji known?
- g. Give a brief historical background of Springfield, Ill.
- h. The word we use for a small enclosed body of water is *lake*. What is the word used by the Germans, the Swedes, and the French for this same thing?

Pictorial Histories

There are many aspects of history to be recorded. There is history recorded so that events are emphasized; there is military history, political history, and cultural history. Perhaps most interesting of all is social history which concentrates on people and tells about how they lived, their manners, and customs. The books by Earle, and the *Early Settlers Series* exemplify this approach. Some social-cultural histories rely on pictures to bring history to life. In addition to works that reproduce photographs from the past, such as *Album of American History,* there are those that feature superb line drawings. The works of Eric Sloane, John Tunis, and Leonard Everett Fisher immediately come to mind. These pictorial histories are closely associated with the social histories because of the contents chosen by these artist-authors. As a type, they are indispensable in the school library media collection.

■ EARLY SETTLER LIFE SERIES, 10 vols. (1981–)*

Contents of the book:

Covers the social life and customs of settlers in the United States. Volume titles provide clues to content area:

Family Home
Schools
Christmas
Loggers and the Sawmill
Settler Children
Stores and Markets

Story Book
Travel
Village Life
Food for the Settler
Activity Guide

Useful characteristics:

1. Heavily illustrated; uses photographs and line drawings.
2. Most illustrations are sepia on cream colored paper.
3. Captions are in colored print.
4. Primary source excerpts (diaries, letters, etc.) are frequent and appear in different typeface with quotation marks so that they stand out for easy identification.
5. Recipes are given in metric measurements.
6. Glossary and small index in each volume.

Skills involved:

1. Concept of primary and secondary sources.
2. Use of subheadings and picture captions.
3. Reading for content.

Developing activities:

1. Choose a volume and leaf through it. Take *Travel* as an example. For each mode of travel described, make a chart showing the advantages and disadvantages of each. For example, steamboats had comfortable interiors, but the engines had a habit of blowing up.
2. Using primary source excerpts find a firsthand description of riding on a corduroy road.
3. Study the rules for students and the rules for teachers given in the *Schools* volume. Have rules changed more for teachers or for students? (You might be surprised!)

*Note: An *Early Settler Activity Guide* volume is an addition to the set. It contains 128 pages of activities and ideas to help the teacher use the set efficiently. As with any guide, the suggestions may be used as presented or they may be adapted to suit individual classroom needs.

■ WORKS OF ERIC SLOANE

Especially useful for the elementary school curriculum are pictorial histories created by Eric Sloane. Among titles to be considered are the following:

Diary of an Early American Boy: Noah Blake—1805
A Museum of Early American Tools
American Yesterday
A Reverence for Wood

Contents of books:

1. Text in the illustration areas is simple enough for the elementary student.
2. In some instances a teacher might need to assist with use of the text.
3. The line drawings are largely self-explanatory.
4. Much social history is woven into these books.

Useful characteristics:

The content and the illustrations.

Skills involved:

The ability to gain information from pictures.

Developing activities:

1. The pictures and the anecdotal text lend themselves to browsing. The book *Reverence for Wood* points out that we still use wood in many important ways, even when we think everything is made of metals and plastic. The book is useful in creating interest, liking, perhaps even reverence in its reader and therefore has a use in ecology units.
2. Using *Reverence for Wood,* find out about *mining* white cedar in New Jersey and why it was done. (Logs had been preserved submerged in swamps.)
3. Discuss the meaning of the expression, "Square peg in a round hole," then find out if square pegs could or could not be used in round holes and why. (They were used to make tighter pegging.)
4. Explain how early wire fences were constructed so that they earned money for the farmer. (Living fruit and nut trees were planted to use as fence posts.)
5. Joseph Jenks used trees as symbols on early American coins he designed. He asked, "What better thing than a tree, to portray the wealth of our country?" Was he correct? Why, or why not?

World History

History takes on increasing importance as the school years proceed. Reference materials for the subject also increase in types and numbers, and as they do, it becomes important to notice their limitations of scope, and their emphases of time and place, or aspect. These characteristics become apparent to students as they use specialized history references.

■ EMERGENCE OF MAN, 11 vols. (1974)

Contents of books:

Titles of the individual volumes indicate the content as follows:

Life Before Man
The First Farmers
The Missing Link
The First Americans
The Metalsmiths
The First Men
The Neanderthals
The Sea Traders
Cro-Magnon Man
The First Cities
The Monument Builders

Useful characteristics:

1. Many colored photographs.
2. Black-and-white line drawings are used for details.
3. Some maps are included.
4. Timeline included in each volume.
5. Cumulative index volume.

Skills involved:

1. Alphabetizing.
2. Use of index.
3. Ability to comprehend relationships.

Developing activities:

1. Select interesting words in the index for fact finding practice. For example, using the *Sea Traders* volume, one could ask the student to explain who the Phoenicians were. Once the article is found, follow-up questions might be developed such as, "What did these peddlers peddle?"
2. A more challenging question might be: "How did people get to the island of Motya from Sicily?" Follow-up with a question about what the causeway proves.

■ ENCYCLOPEDIA OF DISCOVERY AND EXPLORATION, 18 vols. (1971)

Contents of books:

Volume titles indicate the divisions and extent of content:

First Explorers
Beyond the Horizon
Great Age of Exploration
God, Gold, and Glory
Lands of Spice and Treasure
Rivers of Destiny
Charting the Vast Pacific
Bridging a Continent
Jungle Rivers and Mountain Peaks
Lands of the Southern Cross
Seas of Sand
Challenge of Africa
Heartland of Asia
Frozen World
Secrets of the Sea
Roof of the World
The Moon and Beyond

Useful characteristics:

1. Cumulative index volume for set and a short index in each voulme.

2. Primary source excerpts throughout.
3. Appendix features biographies of individual explorers, a glossary, and some old maps reproduced.
4. Well-illustrated, mostly in color.

Skills involved:

1. Alphabetizing.
2. Using letter codes to identify volumes from the cumulative index.
3. Reading for content.

Developing activities:

1. Standard, traditional assignments related to routes, explorers, and their exploits.
2. Potential for good use of primary sources. Volume 16 includes a mountain climbing article that describes how Georges Sonnier fell into a crevasse and was stranded for eight days and seven nights. His account upon rescue is quoted.

Biographical References

People make history; therefore, biographical information is one of the most commonly used types of information. While encyclopedias and dictionaries supply biographical data on many people, both living and dead, these entries represent only a small fraction of the people for whom biographical information is available and wanted.

Individual books of biography are both interesting and useful. They are, as a genre, a part of literature and language arts. Some differentiation needs to be made between biography and autobiography. This is an excellent time to introduce the concept of primary and secondary sources. However, the information supplied in an individual biography may be considerably more than is needed at the time. What is wanted might be found in a collected biography much more easily and quickly.

Sources of collected biography tend to be specialized. One of the important realizations for students is the need to match a specialization with the person about whom information is being sought. To use these references effectively, it is helpful to know the correct spelling of the person's name, the nationality, the profession, and the date span of the life. It is by these descriptors that the biographical collections are made. It is unproductive to expect a book to contain information that it clearly sets out to omit. It is much more desirable to know that reference books have specific content limitations and to provide assistance in selecting appropriate references.

Students should become familiar with the cumulative biographical indexes. Their use avoids missing entries or having to check carefully that a volume was not overlooked when it was being used by someone else. Also, time is not wasted with possible sounding titles, the contents of which are delimited in some unrecognized way.

There are some biographical references that are general. Their coverage includes persons both living and dead, from all countries, and working in all professions. Because these are *general* references, and because the coverage is broad, only the most important people will be included. As the geographic area, discipline, and date span are narrowed, (only Italian photographers of the twentieth century, for example), the chances of finding a person's name increases. However, making the correct reference "match" becomes even more important when the contents becomes increasingly specialized.

These biographical indexes are useful to the extent that the books indexed are found in the school library media center collection. It does not mean that every title will have been purchased, but certainly those that will support the bulk of the curricular needs must be available if the index is to be of real curricular value.

Many collected biography sets have supplements. This is another point the student must understand. People continue to become bona fide candidates for inclusion in the reference book after the publisher's cutoff date. Supplements are normally used to update a work until some years pass and a fully revised edition of the work becomes desirable.

Other biographical references include an assortment of special features. These may be lists by professions, necrologies, or cumulated indexing. *Current Biography* employs all of these. The cumulated indexing increases annually throughout a ten-year period (by decades). Additionally, there is a separate thirty-year index covering 1940–1970.

The McGraw-Hill Encyclopedia of World Biography, Webster's Biographical Dictionary, Facts About the Presidents, Asimov's Biographical Encyclopedia of Science and Technology, Baker's Biographical Dictionary of Musicians, Current Biography, Something About the Author, Junior Book of Authors, the *Concise Dictionary of American Biography, Notable American Women,* and *Twentieth-century American Nicknames,* will be considered indispensable in many elementary school collections.

Periodicals are another source of biographical information. The Wilson *Biography Index,* usually available in junior and senior high schools and public libraries, is a useful means of locating biographical information in periodicals. Choice articles discovered by using this index could be copied and placed in the vertical file for repeated use. There is really no end to the biographical materials available, and much more is being published all the time.

■ LINCOLN LIBRARY OF SPORTS CHAMPIONS, 20 vols. (3rd ed., 1981)

Contents of book:

Biographical information about male and female stars. Includes pictures of the athlete, often engaged in the sport.

Useful characteristics:

1. Cumulative index in last volume.
2. Table of contents in each volume lists athletes alphabetically under their sport.
3. Sports represented by sport symbol.
4. Especially useful for younger students is the summary printed in larger type and easier vocabulary at the start of each entry.
5. A sports terms glossary is found in the last volume.

Skills involved:

1. Alphabetizing.
2. Categorizing by sport.
3. Reading with comprehension.

Developing activities:

1. Given a list of three athletes in the same sport, the student could be asked to put them in sequence chronologically by some aspect of their careers such as number of teams played for or championships earned, etc.
2. Choose names unfamiliar to students because of date, nationality, or sport (such John McGraw, Suzanne Lenglen, or Frank Gotch) and have the students identify the athlete's contribution to the sport.

■ PEOPLE WHO MADE AMERICA, 21 vols. (1973)

Contents of book:

Collected short biographies of "notable men and women of many races and viewpoints from earliest times to the present who helped influence and form the America we live in today."

Useful characteristics:

1. Colored portraits for each person set against a background related to their reputations.
2. Alphabetical arrangement.
3. Volume 21 is a cumulative subject index giving professions, ethnic backgrounds, and categories such as "Women."
4. Approximately fifty pages of fact finding activities after subject index.
5. Entries include lesser-known people as well as old favorites.

Skills involved:

1. Alphabetizing.
2. Fact finding.
3. Note taking.
4. Categorizing.

Developing activities:

1. Give students a group of names and ask them to find out what the people have in common.
2. For a given occupation, students could name an early innovator and a recent practitioner.
3. For the most part, students will be looking for additional information about persons whose names appear in ongoing curriculum.

■ SOMETHING ABOUT THE AUTHOR, 36 vols. (1971–)

Contents of book:

Biographical information about writers and illustrators of books for young people. Portraits of the authors and illustrators are included and sample illustrations from books are reproduced.

Useful characteristics:

1. Indexing is cumulative and includes references to author information found in *Contemporary Authors* and in *Yesterday's Authors of Books for Children.*
2. Cumulative indexing printed on blue pages.
3. Cross-references list other articles in the series in which the person is mentioned.
4. Arrangement within volume is alphabetic by name; pseudonyms are given at start of an article.
5. Articles give information under categorical headings.
6. Small bibliographies lead one to additional sources of information about the writers and illustrators.

Skills involved:

1. Alphabetizing.
2. Use of multiple indexes within a single volume.
3. Use of volume codings and cross-reference codings in cumulative indexes.
4. Use of subheadings.
5. Use of picture captions.
6. Reading for content.

Developing activities:

1. Can be used to provide information regarding the author and/or illustrator for book reports.
2. Caution: Be sure students use the proper index. The authors and illustrators are listed in separate indexes and they are next to each other, A-Z and A-Z. However, they are not interchangeable and care must be taken not to confuse them.

■ WEBSTER'S BIOGRAPHICAL DICTIONARY (1976)

NOTE: Although there are 1980 and 1983 editions of the work under the title *Webster's New Biographical Dictionary,* the use of the reference remains substantially the same.

Contents of book:

Brief biographical sketches, including pronunciation of names, for more than forty thousand individuals from all eras, all professions, and all parts of the world.

Useful characteristics:

1. Dates, important accomplishments, and person's influence on history given in easily understood words and figures.
2. Pronouncing list of international prenames (given names) included.
3. Chronological tables listing United States presidents, vice-presidents, justices of the Supreme Court, members of the Cabinet, signers of the Declaration of Independence and of the Articles of Confederation, delegates to the Constitutional Convention, and members of the Hall of Fame for Great Americans.
4. Chronological tables listing heads of state for the countries of the world.

Skills involved:

1. Alphabetizing.
2. Using chronological listings.
3. Using abbreviations.
4. Looking up person by last name.
5. Looking for proper given name when there are multiple listings of a last name.
6. Recognizing importance of dates when two names are identical.
7. Using "see" references to locate actual entries.

Developing activities:

1. For initial experiences, choose names that are easily identified, and for whom the accomplishment is something the student can comprehend. For example, Marcus Daly, John Muir, or Carl Sandburg.
2. For more advanced experiences, choose names that require differentiation among names. For example, ask the student to find when George Smith, the American geologist, lived. The student would have to find the section for Smith, then the George Smiths, and finally the proper George Smith by skimming the entries. Also note the difference in format when entering individuals with the same last name when they are related to each other as a family.
3. To provide practice in using cross-references, choose a name such as Samuel Miller. The "see" reference sends the user to

the entry Miller, Edward. Here, because the people are related they are listed together within the same entry. Ask the student to name their professions and the relationship between the two men. Again, note the difference in entering individuals with the same last name when they are related and when they are unrelated.

Periodicals and Newspapers

Periodicals are published at regular intervals. Some appear daily, others weekly, monthly, quarterly, or annually. The term *periodical* is preferred over *magazine* because not all periodicals, strictly speaking, are magazines, while all magazines are periodicals.

While the elementary school student will usually not be needing the scholarly, esoteric, or trade publications that interest the advanced student, they do use the periodicals especially designed for them plus a small number of adult periodicals such as the news weeklies, *National Geographic,* and certain ones devoted to hobbies.

The major problem with periodicals in elementary schools has been the lack of storage space for back issues. Without a well-organized, readily available file of some size it is difficult to provide the necessary hands-on experience of following indexing leads to their periodical sources. As yet, few elementary schools have begun microform collections, although the use of a microfiche reader is quite simple and the machinery is not too expensive.

Nonetheless, back files for even a very few titles will provide the students with needed awareness and indexing experiences. The most useful periodical index for elementary school students is *Children's Magazine Guide: Subject Index to Children's Magazines*. It is a monthly publication. Its indexing format is similar to *Reader's Guide to Periodical Literature,* which makes an easy transition when the time comes. The quality of children's periodicals has risen sharply, and many of them include valuable information unavailable elsewhere. The list of titles indexed includes such juvenile weekly newspapers as *Newstime* and *My Weekly*

Reader, and other titles such as, *Boys' Life, Jack and Jill, Cricket, Highlights for Children, Ranger Rick,* and *Arizona Highways*. The index lists stories, poems, and plays as well as factual material.

Students can be introduced to the *National Geographic Index* as most schools do seem to have acquired back issues of that periodical. Other periodicals also produce their own annual indexing and may be used successfully to introduce the concept that periodicals contain current or recent information and that indexing makes retrieval of information from back issues practical. If standard periodical indexes are used, the school library media center's subscription list should match the indexing in so far as possible. Helpful worksheets and workbook pamphlets for teaching the use of periodical indexing are available from both *Subject Index to Children's Magazines* and *Reader's Guide to Periodical Literature*.

Newspapers also have a place in the elementary school library media center. Numerous activities can be developed based on articles and on the format of newspapers. Usually the local paper is available, and sometimes one of broader coverage, such as *USA Today,* is subscribed to. The three great national papers, the *New York Times,* the *Christian Science Monitor,* and the *Wall Street Journal* wait, along with their indexing, for secondary school introduction. These titles are available in microform, and at times they are offered in selected date spans covering a frequently studied school curricular topic. Additionally, there are collections of reproduced front pages published in book form. These also permit the development of newspaper awareness and the improvement of their use. These books are not beyond the scope or budget of the usual elementary school.

Collection Development

Not all school library media centers will be equipped with the materials needed for activities designed to develop student search skills. Specific titles are not as important as types of materials, although certain titles are especially useful in accomplishing learning objectives for the students.

There are some reference books—sets of encyclopedias, for example—that are, by tradition, included in all elementary school library media collections. However, additional sources must be available to support an active skills program. These include specialized reference titles often thought of as being too difficult for an elementary school population, plus a sizable nonfiction collection that supports curriculum topics. A title that is placed in reference in one school library media center may very well be classified for circulation in another. There are many criteria that determine the reference/nonreference decision. The size of the collection, the number of additional titles held on the same topic, conditions of acquisition such as high cost or special memorial gift, likelihood of theft, but especially the type of curricular program use made of the materials, will determine their placement. When ongoing assignments require students to use certain materials frequently, they need to remain on the school library media center shelves throughout the day, and are therefore designated as reference materials.

Reference materials may be circulated overnight, thereby meeting borrowers' needs. Obviously, some problems of nonreturn can occur, but these can be kept under control by revoking the overnight borrowing privilege for the erring student, by peer pressure exerted by classmates in need of the material, or by a phone call to a parent to bring the materials to school immediately. In the case of illness, there are siblings or neighbors at the bus stop who could return the overnight loan materials. Usually the advantages outweigh the disadvantages of maintaining a policy of overnight loan of reference materials. This is really no different than the overnight reference collection created by a reserve system.

Purchasing titles on related topics produced by the same publisher and sharing a common format can be helpful in developing instructional activities. When this type of material is available, and when the assignment is structured in such a way that students are looking for the same types of information, students can interact and help each other while working on individual assignments.

If young students are to be encouraged to seek information, it follows that the school library media collection must contain adequate materials at their reading level. Sometimes the youngest students are limited to an easy collection made up entirely of fiction. In these instances, easy reading nonfiction may be located in an area limited to access by older students. The best practice is to shelve the easy reading nonfiction in an area adjacent to the picture books, within the area accessible to beginning readers. If this is not possible, the easy reading nonfiction books can be pulled and placed in a reserve section, or on a booktruck, for at least the duration of a unit of study.

When a high priority is placed on developing search skills and integrating these skills into the school curriculum, an equally high priority needs to be placed on purchasing nonfiction at all reading levels. Having an adequate supply of support materials will foster this type of teaching/learning activity.

It is not necessary to have a book for each student on every topic studied. However, materials related to a topic of study must be handled in such a way that equal access is assured. A reserve shelf restricted to overnight sign-out, rather than the usual first-come-first-served policy, might be established. Another method useful in making materials serve more students effectively is to encourage classroom teachers to plan together so that not all classrooms of one grade level need the same materials at the same time. Even when the same time period and subject content is being studied, one group could use a biographical approach while another used a geographical approach. Similar plans can be worked out so that fiction, short story, and poetry books—some of which are often in short supply—can be shared successfully. Cooperating and planning among classroom teachers and with the school library media teacher helps make possible the type of search experiences described in these pages even when materials are somewhat limited.

Computer Software—Another Aspect of Collection Development

Computers are now standard equipment in many elementary school library media centers. Their management and use for instructional purposes in the center has become the school library media teacher's responsibility. Sometimes aides and volunteers help with the task, but in the end it is the professional's attitudes that determine quite largely the use made of this medium.

In some cases, the center may be simply the point of distribution and the actual use of the machines will take place in classrooms. More often, however, individual students or small groups of students will be dispatched from classrooms to the center to use the computers for specific time periods and specific program applications. There may be several different brands of computers, or there may be just one. This, plus the software that has been purchased, will determine the extent to which skills practice programs are available.

The school library media teacher who is involved in administering a program of computer usage will surely order some of the better software offering library—that is, learning and reference search—skills practice. The problems and the benefits are just the same for this area of learning as for any other. All software must be previewed because the quality of programs varies widely. However, there are some programs of substantial value that support and reinforce what the school library media teacher has been presenting in the classroom or the school library media center sessions.

No matter how hard a teacher tries when presenting material, there will always be some students who do not "connect" and some aspects of the lesson that pass unlearned. The use of computerized library skills programs can help with this problem. The differences in format and presentation may be the key. Simple repetition may be what is needed, or there may be a different aspect of the topic that is picked up in the computerized atmosphere. The instant feedback on accuracy or the competitive challenge of scoring that is provided in some programs may prove more effective than classroom discussion. The role of the school library media teacher is in no way diminished, but rather complemented, by the use of these programs. Both are needed for best results. Differences in learning/teaching styles—not only between classroom and computer but among programs available—have impact. Computerized programs can enhance and reinforce what the student is learning.

Children may use the programs individually, either in free or assigned time. Small groups from a classroom may be sent to work together on specific programs. Many children have computer access within their own homes. Some are imbued with the games attitude, while others are bored stiff with a program of limited scope. A good choice of software is the key to successful use of computers.

Programs that reward the "wrong" answer with an appealing sound or picture response have been found to encourage children who enjoy those responses to give incorrect answers. Some manufacturers have changed their approach by greeting incorrect responses with quiet and correct answers with game type scoring charts. Sometimes these appear to take up a good deal of time, and when they can not be bypassed optionally, a student may be completely turned off by the program. Certainly, there could be considerably more substantive material to be used and practiced within the limited amount of computer time the students have available to them if some of these "interruptions" were omitted or minimized. For some students they may be an attractive feature but for others they are a deterrent. Matching the student with the program is essential.

We have seen excellent use being made of the library skills presentations by *Right On Programs*. Fourth and fifth graders enjoy their use, gain a better grasp of card catalog subject heading choices, and can review dictionary skills. *Answering Questions Library Style* offers ten categories, among them subject terminology, drawer letter spans, finding books on the shelf, and finding facts within a text. The *Library Skills* programs offer a speed control feature that permits the user to adjust the response times to personal preference. Word processing programs such as *Bank Street Writer* or *Magic Slate* have made differences in learning to write more effectively in the early grades. They have also made the publishing of school or class newspapers a much simpler project.

Other utility discs simplify the designing of the teacher's practice material. It is no longer necessary to engage in programming in order to make effective use of a computer as a teaching/learning tool. A program such as *Catalogit* is an example utility discs for student use. One elementary school library media teacher has plans to use a very simple catalog card-making program with fifth graders. Her idea is that if these students can create a first level of descriptors themselves, they will then be able to use those they find in the card catalog more effectively.

This activity would be one in which students would participate on their own time, and which would capitalize on the students' fascination with the computer. For this school library media teacher's own use she has chosen *Catalog Card and Label Writer, version 4,* (1984). The use of computerized skills programs does not diminish the role of the school library media teacher because the students are experiencing contact with the material at another level and are cooperating among themselves.

By the time this book is published there will be substantially more and improved software available, but the problem of making good choices will be no easier. Although the general practice is not to send computer software out for preview, local firms may be found that provide previewing opportunities and these are worth looking for. With careful previewing and evaluating there can be little doubt that a collection of computerized library and search skills programs will be worth their cost and the students' time.

PART THREE
TEACHING THE RESEARCH PROCESS

Effective Instruction

Two basic ideas about what provides effective instruction permeate the activities cited in this book. First, nothing—no item of interest or information—can be too small to spark an effective learning experience; and second, a number of smaller assignments that provide suitable practice of skills are more effective than one major assignment. Just as one does not learn any other skill through a single exposure without subsequent practice or application, the skills associated with the location and use of information require varied and extended practice in using them.

Schoolwide activities or contests, well-planned learning centers, or involvement bulletin boards, as well as search activities, can be pleasurable to children as well as educationally effective. Any little thing can spark learning activity, provided that the teacher—including the school library media teacher—is alert about following it up. For example, the words *whole* and *hole* turned into schoolwide learning experiences at the start of a "whole new school year." The word *fire;* its multiple meanings; aspects of fire safety information; history of fire fighting; scientific concepts of ignition, burning, and extinguishing of fire; as well as Benjamin Franklin's contributions, provided another schoolwide experience.

The sooner a student can effectively learn independently, the sooner that student can assume increased responsibility for self-directed and continuing learning. It is with this thought in mind that some programs for gifted students concentrate on providing basic search and information processing skills at an earlier than usual age. This allows them to go full speed ahead on their own and to pursue individual interests, freed from lockstep instruction.

Students need to learn how to use a source once they find it. To do this, they must have hands-on experience. It is not enough to tell them that the reference has multiple indexes. They need assigned activities that offer sufficient structure to help them to use the tool. Just talking about books does not permit a *process* to be learned. Answers might be repeated accurately enough for a pencil-and-paper type test, but often without total comprehension or understanding of application. Too often facts are given about the sources, but the opportunity to interact with the material is lacking.

Textbook or workbook "library skills" units require every child to answer the same questions using the same reference sources. Answers will be identical. In a very short time, student "deals" are made, and only some children actually experience the instructional intent of the assignment. When each child has a different subject topic, the answers will be different, although finding them requires the same search technique and skills. Even though the same reference titles will be used, most children will actually have to do the planned search work. Far better results will be obtained when the school library media teacher devises worksheets tailored to the center's holdings, to students' needs, and to teachers' intentions. It is well worth the added effort to create your own worksheets and use commercially prepared or other identical ones for initial group instruction. The mere assigning of a different letter of the alphabet to be used by each student when selecting a topic will go a long way toward accomplishing this goal even when stock format and questions are used.

It takes different skills to read for content than to read for story line. Too often, basal reading selections are mostly narration. The students are taught decoding skills, word attack skills, and comprehension of the story line. Additionally, they need to differentiate between fact and opinion, be able to use textual aids such as black headings, italics, picture captions, charts, graphs, and tables. They need to be able to find materials in different sources and see if they say the same thing. If the sources do not agree, then the student then must learn how to handle differences of opinion, interpretations, and facts.

Important skills to be learned include using indexes, fact finding, using headings and subheadings in text, note taking, outlining, organization of ideas, and the acknowledgment of sources, first in bibliographies and later in footnotes.

Textbooks are often used for reading assignments and answering chapter-end questions. If the classroom teacher structures the questions adequately, textbooks can be used to begin the higher order thought processes. However, the wide range of types of references to be found in a school library media center makes it a necessary continuation laboratory, carrying on from where the textbook leaves off.

The closely integrated classroom/school library media program is not workable when the students are in contact with library staff and resources only once a week during a prescribed half hour. It takes administrative support to insist that the school library media center be open rather than shut off through scheduling. Students need to be able to come to the center from their classrooms as the need arises. The classroom teachers should be able to use the center for small group or entire classroom workshops. Sometimes these sessions call for a planned presentation by the school library media teacher; at other times (after initial instruction has been provided) the role is one of providing informal support. Sometimes a small group will go to the center to work with the school library media teacher while another group of students remains to work with the teacher in the classroom. It takes perseverance, but even schools that have become accustomed to using library media resources only through scheduled class sessions can be changed. They can discover that with the open approach, each classroom receives increased, as well as more effective, service from the school library media teacher and the center.

Structure is very important. The youngest students want to emulate the "big kids," but they have not yet decided that assignments are of necessity "boring." Bruner's concept can be used effectively in developing activities: i.e., that if information is structured in little bits, even the youngest students can succeed in grasping it. They do not have to be held back. Through careful choice of examples and by making certain that a sufficient number of instructional examples are worked through with the group, the groundwork is done that makes the total project a happy, successful one.

The hierarchy of skills needed to carry out an assignment deserves attention. The student can not move on without having

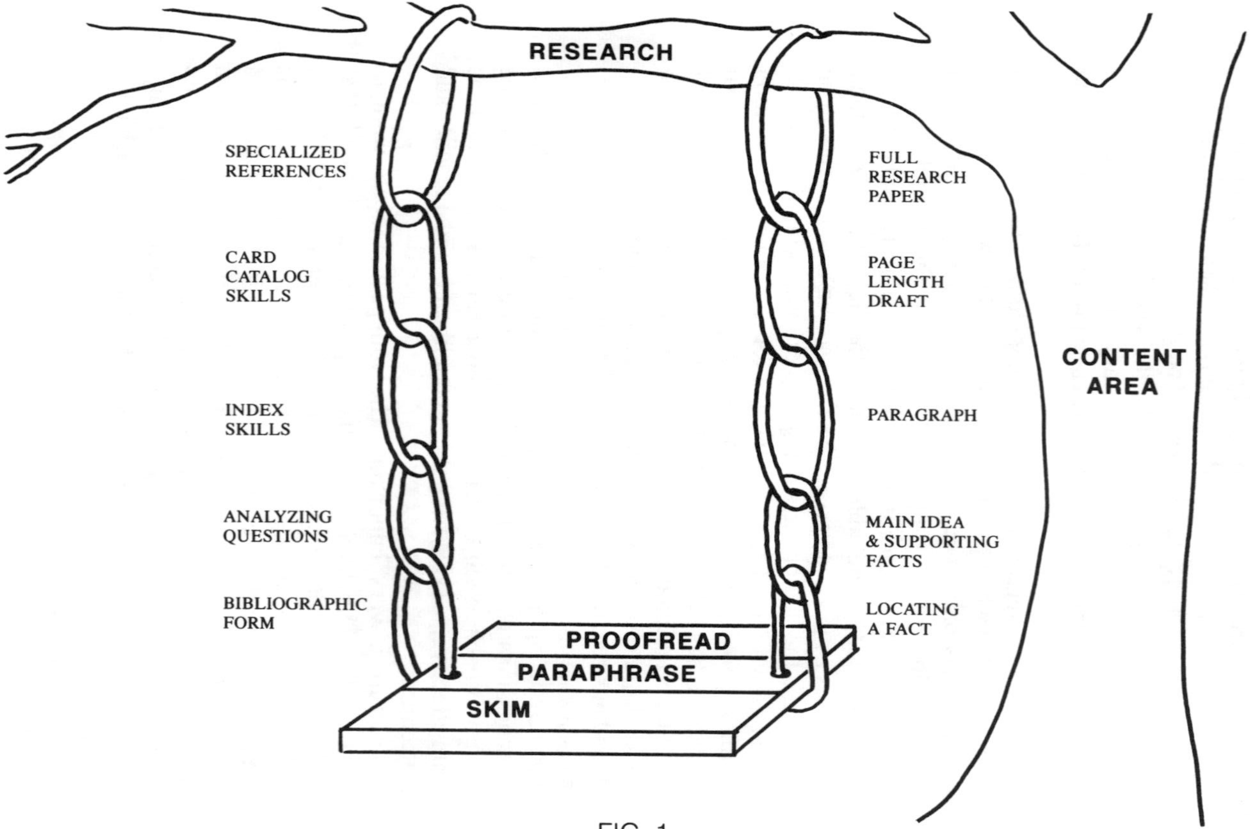
RESEARCH
SPECIALIZED REFERENCES
CARD CATALOG SKILLS
INDEX SKILLS
ANALYZING QUESTIONS
BIBLIOGRAPHIC FORM
FULL RESEARCH PAPER
PAGE LENGTH DRAFT
PARAGRAPH
MAIN IDEA & SUPPORTING FACTS
LOCATING A FACT
CONTENT AREA
PROOFREAD
PARAPHRASE
SKIM

FIG. 1

mastered the needed preceding skills (see Fig. 1). The skills can be taught separately. To write a report the student must have learned to locate information, take notes, and identify main ideas and supporting evidence. There must be evaluation, selection, and reorganization of ideas for presentation. Bibliographies must be prepared. Each of these skills needs to have been learned one-by-one, built on, and developed sufficiently so that when put together, a significant project can be carried out. An approach that structures each step, with one step leading to another, is much more likely to be successful than one where a paper is assigned, and little or no advance preparation for working on it has been done with the students.

Only the teacher who continues to think, to choose, to search; a teacher who is comfortable with the risk taking of decision making, can transmit these process skills to students. This is true whether the teacher is based within the school library media center or the classroom. However, the eager school library media teacher must remember that some styles of teaching and managing classrooms are more conducive to use of the center than others. Teachers who tend to use learnings centers and small group interaction within the classroom tend to allow, even encourage, students to make use of the school library media center. Teachers who like to stand up and talk to the entire class do not. This is a philosophical matter. There is so much to teach and so little time in which to do it. The first type of classroom teacher sees the center as an aid in teaching what is to be taught and the school library media teacher as a partner. The second type of classroom teacher tends to see the center as a competitor for students' time. To them, student time spent in the library media center is time off task. For the students assigned to these teachers, alternatives need to be established so that the students may have access to the services and materials of the center. Time before school, after school, during recess must be made available. For them, schoolwide contests, learning centers, involvement bulletin boards, and even a mouse house take on added importance.

The nature of the assignments teachers make has tremendous impact on learning opportunity. Is the teacher interested in the product or process? A student may be asked to write a paragraph on a topic. If only the completed first draft is considered for the grade, the student develops a tendency to find a source and copy it—especially when the teacher finds this type of activity satisfactory. In contrast, an assignment that calls for turning in note cards, a rough draft, and a final revision complete with bibliography—with each segment graded and contributing to the final grade—communicates the importance of learning the *process*. It is the process that allows the student to experience educational growth. Learning a handful of facts that quickly become outdated is of considerably less value to the students' educational and intellectual development.

Locating Facts

The initial search skill that needs to be introduced, practiced, and developed is fact finding. This can be begun as soon as the student can read with comprehension—as early as first grade. The concept of a *fact* needs clarification. The dictionary suggests that a fact is "a thing that has actually happened, or is true," "the state of things as they are," and "something said to have occurred or supposed to be true." For the purposes of research with young students, it proves effective to explain to them that a fact is a piece of information and that it can be an answer to a question. Questions that may be used as examples are: "How big is it?" "What does it look like?" "Where is it found?" "Where does it live?" "How is it used?" "How does it move?", etc. The questions need to be related to the topic that is being investigated.

The first time a student attempts this sort of activity, the expectation should be to find just one fact. The expectation grows as the skills of the students grow and as the complexities of the materials being used increase.

A problem often overlooked is that fact finding is very difficult for beginning students. Waiting until they are older does not eliminate the problem. The beginner, of whatever age, needs to be guided and assisted in recognizing needed information when and where it is found. This does not happen automatically. It is a skill that can be begun quite early and is an essential building block for successfully completing standard assignments.

Classroom teachers sometimes make assignments which require a learning sophistication on the part of students that has not been developed. Preparation is essential. Upper grade elementary school students continue to have difficulty with these simple search skills if they have never had appropriate instruction and the opportunity for practice. Care must be taken not to assume that students have these basic skills. It is easy to take for granted that skills which are automatic for the teacher have been learned by the student. Because students read fluently and with comprehension does not mean that they can identify what they have read as the fact they are looking for. As incongruous as this may seem to an adult, it is true. Moreover, when teacher assumptions lead to oversight in this matter, the student remains handicapped until the omission is corrected. While this skill of recognizing facts and selecting the needed fact can be introduced in first grade, and mastered by some students, it may very well need to be reviewed or retaught throughout the upper grades if mastery is to be achieved by the less able student.

SAMPLE ACTIVITIES FOR FACT FINDING PRACTICE

Create sample passages that contain facts without distractors for initial fact finding experiences. Using the who-what-when-why-where format (not always in that sequence) simple news story-type paragraphs can be created quite easily.

The following paragraphs can be put onto a transparency and projected one at a time. Students are asked to read the paragraph and identify the five Ws. Answers are shared through class discussion. As many paragraphs as are needed for student practice can be created.

Who What When Where Why Activity

The Brown family lost their home to a fire.
It happened the night of October 3.
The fire was caused by faulty wiring.
Nobody was hurt, but the family lost their belongings.
They will rebuild this Washington, D.C. house.

Quintuplets were born on October 1 to Mary and John Smith.
The three boys and two girls are all doing well.
They will be going home next week to join their big brother in their suburban Chicago home.

A new drug has been developed by the Lilly Company.
The drug will be used to treat chicken pox.
It will be available to doctors across the country in January.

A recurring problem in the school library media center is overdue books.
A few students keep ignoring their names on the room lists.
Students who keep this up will not be happy.

The following activity requires skimming to find facts because the book series used (*Early Career Books* series) has minimal indexing. Students read the question, determine the appropriate career field (book), and leaf through to find the specific career within the book. There is a one-page photograph of an individual engaged in the job and an accompanying page of text. The student skims the page of text to find the specific information asked for in the question. Questions can be devised either one per book in the series or several per book depending upon the number of students participating.

Career Book Questions

Answer a minimum of five questions. Share the books.

1. What does a counter agent for an airline have to do?
   a.
   b.
   c.
   d.
2. What does a frameman do for the telephone company?
3. What does a police rescue unit bomb squad member need to know?
   How does a bomb squad member dress?
4. What does a proofreader do in the printing process?
   a.
   b.
   What word is misspelled in the sample sentence to be proofread?
5. What do packaging engineers do for computer companies?
   What must they know?
6. What does a concessions manager do for a hockey team?
   a.
   b.
7. What is an equipment manager's job for a baseball team?
   a.
   b.
   How many uniforms does he have to keep clean?

An activity that calls for a higher level, more developed ability to locate specific facts within a book is one that uses the *In America* series on immigrants published by Lerner. Each title in this series discusses the contributions of a particular nationality as immigrants to the United States. This activity calls for reading picture captions and skimming the text to locate the contribution identified in the question. The final step is to read the section to identify the name of the person needed to answer the question.

Immigrant Contributors

Find the name of the individual that fits the description given in the question. There will be only one person taken from each book in the series.

1. Name the individual of German descent who designed the Brooklyn Bridge.
2. Name the French descendent who was the inventor of the semiautomatic rifle used by the United States Army during World War II.
3. Name the Hungarian descendent who isolated and identified vitamin C.
4. Name the Swedish descendent who founded the Greyhound Bus Lines.
5. Name the Mexican golfer who was named sportsman of the year in 1971.
6. Name the Scots naturalist who helped establish the national parks system in the United States.
7. Name the Chinese descendent who was the highest paid cameraman in Hollywood and who won Oscars for *Hud* and *The Rose Tattoo*.
8. Name the Polish woman who created renewed interest in the harpsichord and its music.
9. Name the architect of Czech descent who designed the Gothic spires of St. Patrick's Cathedral in New York City.
10. Name the conductor from India who was the youngest conductor ever to lead a major symphony orchestra.

CONFLICTS: TERMINOLOGY AND USE OF RESERVES

Beginning searchers are often troubled by terminology. The interchangeablility of terms used in the titles of reference books is one example: encyclopedia, dictionary, handbook, and glossary or yearbook, factbook, and almanac. Content terminology is just as varied when one considers the terms story, folktale, legend, or myth.

Titles of books do not necessarily use the same interpretation of vocabulary that classroom instructors use. In a curriculum that differentiates between fairy tales and folktales, it is important to provide the student with a clear-cut set of criteria to use. Editors do not use these same criteria when writing or giving titles to books. This can create problems with teachers' directions and assignments unless there is teamwork between the classroom teacher and the school library media teacher. This is especially true when using general and specialized encyclopedias. If the teacher prohibits students from using an *encyclopedia*—meaning a general encyclopedia only—the student will refuse to use a specialized resource simply because the word *encyclopedia* appears in the title. There must be communication and understanding of purpose and language.

Another problem can arise when the reserve collection becomes a classroom collection or is on a booktruck that is rolled into the classroom. Care must be taken by the classroom teacher to keep the materials on the booktruck, and get the booktruck back to the school library media center as soon as the class session using these materials is completed. Sometimes, when materials are on a portable reserve booktruck and out of the center for a period, other students will be sent to the center to use those same materials. As obvious a complication as this is, it does happen. Also, when materials are taken to the classroom, students may place materials in their desks instead of back on the booktruck. A reserve collection in the classroom requires added vigilance from the teacher if the materials are to remain available to that class and to others who may be sharing the reserve collection. Similar problems may arise even when the reserve collection remains in the school library media center. Individual responsibility becomes more important when reserve collections are created. The purpose of reserve collections is to eliminate conflict and to make the materials available to more students more of the time. This does not happen without cooperation by everyone—students and teachers alike.

Bibliographies

When students locate information in a reference source, it is just as important to identify the source as it is to take down the information. Young students need to understand that they are using someone else's thoughts when they are writing down information from a reference source. The idea that copying word-for-word is really stealing that person's ideas needs to be communicated to the students. There is no problem with this when classroom teachers refuse to accept plagiarized work. Requiring a bibliography as a part of a completed research project is essential. Students shoud be introduced to the correct format from the very beginning. When all teachers in a school system, or at least within a building, agree upon a common form and require its use, students are not faced with the problem of multiple bibliography formats which vary from teacher to teacher. While style sheets exhibit some variation in terms of punctuation, the basic sequence of information is standard.

One does not need to wait until students have reached the level of sophistication in their written work at which they cite footnotes in order to insist that they provide their sources in a bibliography. The transition to footnotes should be made as soon as the student's skills warrant it in secondary school.

One method for introducing the writing of bibliographic form to young students is to include correct bibliographic citations in the book report format. The standard bibliographic format can be presented in class sessions. A transparency showing a sample title page is used to provide group practice in preparing a bibliographic entry, and individual students can use whatever library book they happen to be reading for additional practice.

Simple annotations can be created for books on a given topic and used as practice in writing correct bibliographic citations. Each annotation includes the necessary information—author, title, place of publishing, publisher, copyright date and pages—in paragraph form. Since there are several citations on the topic, the next step is to arrange them in alphabetic order. Once students are comfortable with citing an individual book, then examples are included which use articles from encyclopedias and periodicals. As need arises, formats for audiovisuals are presented.

SAMPLES OF TEXT TO USE FOR BIBLIOGRAPHY WRITING PRACTICE

DIRECTIONS: Using the information supplied, write bibliography cards, and arrange them alphabetically.

1. In a book published by the National Geographic Society called *Indians of the Americas,* Matthew W. Stirling talks about types of houses on pages 78–93. This book was published in Washington, D.C. in 1955.
2. The 1980 *Worldbook Encyclopedia* has an article called INDIAN, AMERICAN. It is in volume 10 and discusses houses on pages 112–15. This article is written by Merwyn S. Garbarino. This work is published by Worldbook—Childcraft International, Inc. in Chicago.
3. Oliver La Farge's book, *The American Indian,* published by Golden Press in New York in 1960 gives information about houses on pages 15–23.

Note Taking Skills

While fact finding activities can be practiced orally or as a group project, note taking is an individual skill. Locating a fact involves finding it and repeating it. In contrast, note taking requires the student to gather the meanings and to put them into their own words succinctly. It takes practice to reword materials and to determine key concepts which will permit recall of details later when writing the initial draft. It is this that makes note taking difficult to master. It is also what makes teaching the skill a time-consuming and repetitious endeavor.

As soon as students have become able to recognize facts in the written material they are reading, the next step is to learn to write key words and phrases for future reference. In preparation for note taking, students should have experience with assignments which specifically ask that answers be listed only rather than given in complete sentences. There is a time and place for writing in complete sentences; however, it is equally important to learn to write meaningful fragments. When students are asked to take notes, they tend to copy complete sentences, and even paragraphs.

Once the idea of using sentence fragments is implanted, beginning students will select a group of words to take down without comprehension. These words may not be the ones needed to convey the meaning of the passage. This is evidence that they have not yet mastered step one—the identification of a fact. The teacher does not need to wait until fact identification is perfect before introducing note taking. The two skills clarify each other.

Working on the two together, after the initial introduction of fact finding, makes learning these skills easier.

Initial experiences should be structured in such a way that the distractors are limited. This really means choosing examples in which the writing style is sufficiently simplified and structured to assure success. The volumes called "Getting the Facts," from the *Specific Skill* series provides excerpts suitable for beginning note takers. (See the note taking activity that follows.) Although this commercial series is designed to work on comprehension skills in the traditional manner of reading a passage and answering recall questions, the passages are suitable for note taking practice. The following examples use passages from different levels of the series to provide a unit with a built-in increase in degree of difficulty.

For the first two passages the students are asked to give examples that fit a category; for example, types of clocks and how they work or things people have done while sleepwalking. The third passage asks them to take notes on two different topics—where birds' nests are built and what is used to build them. At this level it is important that the students separate notes related to the two topics. In the last passage the students are asked to find information related to three topics. With the third and fourth passages it becomes important to categorize notes in a structured format. In the first two examples, note format is not an important consideration because all of the notes are on the same topic.

To begin this note taking unit each student is provided with a copy of the passages (either a printout or a set of the booklets), and a set of the questions. Questions may be on the printout, written on the board, or projected from a transparency while the students proceed with the activity. The teachers explain that notes are key words and phrases rather than complete sentences copied from the passage. A question is presented and the students are given time to read the passage and write notes that answer the question. Students discuss what they have written down and their work is critiqued in terms of their having used key words and phrases rather than sentences. The first few responses will tend to be complete sentences. However, students quickly learn to re-word their responses.

The teacher moves to the second passage and repeats the procedure. Responses are usually more on target. With the third and fourth passages, discussion regarding format becomes important. Initially, students are directed to use different sections of their paper in order to categorize the notes by topic. The important element at this stage is simply to keep notes for different topics separate from each other. As sophistication increases, traditional outline formats will be introduced.

1. NOTE TAKING ACTIVITY: Four Exercises*

Questions:

1. "Clocks, Clocks, Clocks"
   In notetaking form—that is key words and phrases but not complete sentences—name types of clocks and how they work.
2. "They Walk at Night"
   Take notes on things people have done while sleepwalking.
3. "No Place Like Home"
   Take notes to answer these questions:
   a. Where are bird nests built?
   b. What has been used to build bird nests?
4. "Bells for Ringing"
   Take notes to answer these questions:
   a. What are bells used for?
   b. What are bells made of?
   c. How does a bell make its sound?

*From "Getting the Facts," Specific Skill (Baldwin, N.Y.: Barnell Loft, 1976).

Example 1: "Clocks, Clocks, Clocks"

One clock doesn't make any sound. Yet, it wakes people in the morning. This clock gives off light. The light makes people wake up. Some call it the Light Clock!

Another clock gets people up even faster. This clock gives the one who is sleeping a little shock of electricity. It could be called the Shock Clock!

One clock really tells the time. It calls out the time. This clock says, "five o'clock" or "two o'clock," or whatever the time may be. It's the Talking Clock!

People have to look up to see most clocks. This is not so with one clock in New York. People look down. They see the clock under their feet. It's the Sidewalk Clock!

How would you like to have a Ring Clock? It really doesn't ring. It is called a Ring Clock because you can put it around your finger.

Example 2: "They Walk at Night"

Some people walk in their sleep. They get out of bed and walk around the house. Then they go back to bed. People who walk in their sleep are called sleepwalkers.

Sleepwalkers do funny things. One woman got out of bed and began to cook food. She made a fine meal while still asleep.

Some sleepwalkers even walk out of their homes. One little boy walked out of his house. He walked until he came to a river. Into the water he jumped.

One man got up in the night. He went out and cut down a tree. Back to bed he went. In the morning he got up again. There was the tree on the ground.

People say that sleepwalkers do not get hurt. This is not so. Sleepwalkers can fall. One man fell from the top of his house. He got up on the roof in his sleep!

Example 3: "No Place Like Home"

Birds do not always make their nests in trees or bushes. They don't always use birdhouses. Some birds build their homes in strange places.

One bird used a mailbox to make its home. The letter carrier first found the nest when putting a letter into the box.

Boys and girls sometimes help birds find homes. One boy found a bird living in his baseball glove. The boy had left the glove hanging in a barn near his house. Another bird made its home in a girl's pocketbook. The girl left the open pocketbook on the ground.

A nest was once found in the pocket of a man's suit. The suit had been left on the wash line. Another bird made its nest inside an old tin can. The home for one bird was the top of a train. Each time the train moved, the bird got a free ride.

Nest are sometimes made of more than just sticks and mud. One nest was found with a bubble gum wrapper inside. Another bird used tinsel from a Christmas tree. One bird even used money to make its home. A dollar bill was used to line its nest. It doesn't matter where it is or what it's made of. "There's no place like home," say the birds.

Example 4: "Bells for Ringing"

Bells have many uses. They tell us someone is at the door. They tell us when it is time to wake up. People ring bells when the new year begins. Bells ring when it is time to go to church. Bells sometimes tell us when to eat.

Long ago, bells had even more uses. People rang bells when they had news to tell. They were rung to warn of approaching enemies. Bells were placed around the necks of animals. The sound of the bells told the farmers where the animals had gone. Some farmers still use bells on animals.

Bells are made in the shape of a cup. They are made of wood, glass, and metal. Most often they are made of copper and tin. A piece of metal called a clapper hangs down inside. The clapper hits the side and makes the sound.

The biggest bell ever made was never rung. The bell was as tall as a two-story house. A piece of the bell broke off before it could be used. Later the bell was made into a church. More than forty people could stand inside!

For many, many years people liked to put bells on their shoes and on their ears. As they walked, the little bells would ring. Everyone knew they were coming.

Follow-up experiences can be developed by using passages taken from trade and reference books. Passages are selected both for the difficulty of the writing style and the relevance of the content to ongoing classroom units of study. Note taking skills are thereby integrated into the content areas being studied. The instructional time serves a dual purpose. The classroom unit content is being covered at the same time that the note taking skills are being practiced. Obviously, appropriate selections can be made only when the classroom teacher and the school library media teacher plan together.

Experience has shown that an effective way of developing passages from trade and reference books is to skim the material and note suitable paragraphs. These pages can be duplicated and then cut and pasted to form a master which is then copied for individual student use. Another method is for the classroom teacher or school library media teacher to examine the content of suitable books, choose a few phrases for facts and terminology, and actually write suitable copy themselves. Either way, the passage can be tailored to the developmental level of the students involved.

As a variation to note taking, the students can be asked to underline on their duplicated copy the words they would write down as notes. This relieves boredom but also provides greater practice in the skill of recognizing important facts. If a student has underlined more than key words and phrases, they can go back, reread the passage, and use an alternate symbol such as parentheses or circling to revise their selections.

Another approach is to type a passage in primary size print for projection on a transparency. In this way, student attention can be focused on a portion of a passage. It also allows the teacher to demonstrate what should be included as notes. Don't overlook using headings and line drawings to add visual interest to the materials you create.

2. NOTE TAKING ACTIVITY: Lizards*

Method of presentation:

1. The directions to the students are to take notes on the paragraph giving the facts related to who, what, when, where, and why. The usual response is to give a single fact for each category. This is sufficient for most categories. However, the "what" category, to be complete, requires the noting of a series of facts. In addition, there tends to be a lively discussion over the "when" category. Actually, the passage does not tell "when." The words "when she was five years old" seem to many students to answer the question. Further discussion convinces the students that to answer a "when" question one needs an identifiable point in time. Phrases such as "during the Civil War," "in the Depression years," and "last summer" are shared as examples that identify a specific time.
2. Students are asked to write down or to underline facts about lizards *in general.* The intent is to have them skip over important facts in the passage which relate to a specific kind of lizard. At this stage of development, a number of students will not be able to make this kind of differentiation and will include all important facts in the passage. Through discussion, differentiation is made between facts about lizards in general and facts about specific lizards. Students can then be asked to reread the passage and identify facts about specific lizards.

*From Edward Ricciuti, *Shelf Pets: How to Take Care of Small Wild Animals* (New York: Harper & Row, 1972).

Example 1:

My oldest daughter discovered this in an unexpected manner when she was five years old. We were visiting in Puerto Rico when she found a small anolis lizard, four inches long, on the trunk of a palm tree. She let the little creature run along her arm, and then grasped it in her hand. Something of a comedian, she then held the lizard near her nose, staring it in the eye. The anole promptly bit her on the tip of the nose. My daughter released the lizard, but for twenty seconds or so it hung there, dangling from the end of her nose. Then it let go, dropped to the ground, and scampered away. Fortunately, the lizard's bite left only a small scratch. It also left my dauther with more respect for lizards, small and large.

Example 2:

There are approximately three thousand species of lizards. These reptiles, which belong to the same scientific order as the snakes, have been around for a long time. They probably appeared on Earth more than 180 million years ago, during the time of the dinosaurs. Incidentally, although the name "dinosaur" means "terrible lizard," the dinosaurs were not lizards at all, but belonged to another branch of the reptiles. During the millions of years lizards have existed, they have made their way to all continents except Antarctica, and to many islands. In fact, the world's largest lizards live on the Indonesian islands of Komodo, Flores, Padar, and Rintja. The "komodo monitor" (the monitors are a family of lizards) can grow to a length of ten feet and weigh 250 pounds.

Lizards have made themselves at home in all sorts of habitats, from desert to rain forest. There are lizards that glide through the air, lizards that scamper about the trees, lizards that burrow underground, lizards that swim in the sea, and even lizards—the basilisks of tropical America—that can run on the surface of water. Some lizards feed on plant materials, but most are carnivorous. In captivity, many of the latter require live food such as crickets and earthworms.

3. NOTE TAKING ACTIVITY: Effects of Regional Differences in Africa*

Method of presentation:

1. Make copies of the examples for each student or project the examples using transparencies and an overhead projector.
2. Before having students take individual notes, work as a class group and discuss with them (a) the impact of climate and geography on how one lives, and (b) that Africa is a large area including several different regions.
3. Have students take notes which emphasize effects of climate on life style, and major changes in each region.
4. Discuss each section with the class and verify what notes should have been taken. (Students make corrections on their papers).
5. Have students write a topic sentence and two or three supporting details describing the effects of regional differences in Africa using the notes which have been taken to help with this task.

*From William Allen, Man in Africa (Grand Rapids, Mich.: Fideler, 1972), 27, 28, 37, 42.

Example 1: Northern Africa

About seven thousand years ago, the climate of northern Africa was very different from the climate there today. In many areas, there was enough rainfall to allow grass and even trees to grow. Hunters roamed the forests and grasslands in search of wild animals to kill for food. Herdsmen raised sheep, cattle, and other livestock on the broad, grassy plains.

As time passed, the climate of northern Africa grew drier. The rivers that had flowed there for many years eventually disappeared. The trees and grass withered and died, and much of northern Africa turned into a desert that is now called the Sahara.

Example 2: The Nile Valley

The valley of the Nile River became a productive farming area. When people first came to the Nile Valley, much of the land there was covered with jungles and swamps. Gradually, the people who lived there cleared away the jungles and drained the water off the land. They laid out fields and began to grow crops such as barley and wheat.

The Nile Valley was extremely well suited to farming. Because most of the land was level, it could be cultivated fairly easily with simple farm tools. Although the climate was very dry, the Nile River provided all the water farmers needed for irrigating their crops. In addition, the river contained much soil that had washed down from the highlands of eastern Africa.

Each year, the Nile overflowed its banks and deposited a new layer of rich soil on the land. As a result, the land could be farmed year after year without becoming less fertile. The warm sunshine, the rich soil, and the water from the river helped the farmers in the Nile Valley to produce large amounts of crops.

Example 3: Central Africa

Forest kingdoms grew up along the Gulf of Guinea. At about the same time people were settling in the grasslands south of the Sahara, other Negro people probably journeyed still farther south into the forest region along the Gulf of Guinea.

The dense rain forests in this region protected them from more powerful groups of people and provided them with wood from which they made many useful articles. The hot, humid climate in that part of Africa was good for growing certain crops, such as yams and rice. As we have learned, the rain forests also had large deposits of gold, which the forest people traded for other goods with people who lived to the north.

Example 4: Western Africa

Civilizations began to develop in Africa's western grasslands. The people who settled in the grasslands south of the Sahara had vast, open areas in which to hunt and to farm. They were not forced to live as closely together as the people in the north who settled along the coast or in the narrow Nile Valley. When the population in one area became too large for everyone to farm successfully, or when wild animals became too scarce for the hunters, these early peoples would often move on to another area in the grasslands. Sometimes, part of a group would leave to find new lands and build new villages.

4. NOTE TAKING ACTIVITY: ASTRONOMY*

Method of presentation:

1. Review what skimming is. Emphasize that the student reads for the *key word*.

2. Ask the students to skim the examples which are shown all at once on the overhead projector. Have them write the paragraph number in which the answer to the question is found, and also write the fact that answers the question on their paper.

Questions:

1. What paragraph tells about how rocket engines work? (Paragraph 3)
   What makes the hot gas? (Burning fuel.)
2. What paragraph tells about gravity? (Paragraph 2)
   What must spacecraft do? (Travel faster than gravity's pull.)
3. What paragraph tells about astronomy? (Paragraph 1)
   What did Galileo do first? (Use a telescope.)
4. What paragraph tells about life forms? (Paragraph 5)
   What is an amoeba? (Very simple life form.)
5. What paragraph tells about satellites? (Paragraph 4)
   What cannot bend? (Invisible television waves.)

*Adapted from Patricia Daniels, ed. *Let's Discover Outer Space,* vol. 15 of *Let's Discover* (Milwaukee: Raintree, 1980).

Example 1:

Astronomy is the study of the universe. Astronomers have watched the sun, moon, and stars for hundreds of years. Galileo was the first one to look at the planets through a telescope.

Example 2:

Gravity is a strong force that keeps us on earth. Spacecraft must travel very fast to get free of the pull of gravity. They must fly much faster than jet planes.

Example 3:

Blow up a balloon and let it go. It will fly away as the air rushes out. A rocket engine works the same way. When the fuel burns it makes a hot gas. The gas shoots out and the rocket moves forward.

Example 4:

Invisible waves carry television pictures through the air. These waves travel in straight lines. They can not bend around the earth's surface. The television pictures are sent up to a satellite. It sends them back to another spot on the earth. That is how people in the United States can see a sports event live from Europe.

Example 5:

There are many kinds of life. The amoeba is a tiny, very simple form of life. Flowering plants and mammals are much more complicated life forms. There is life even in difficult places. Cactus plants live in hot, dry deserts. Bacteria can live in the Arctic.

5. NOTE TAKING ACTIVITY: WHAT CAN CURRENT DO?*

Method of presentation:

1. Students are asked to read the first two paragraphs and identify the four effects of electricity. After identifying the four effects their attention is focused on each effect, and notes are taken saying how the effect is produced and citing examples of applications in daily life.
2. Here again, three of these effects cause little difficulty. The heating, luminous, and chemical effects are straightforward in their presentation. However, when the students come to the section on the magnetic effect, they often get off the track and take notes on permanent and temporary magnets. While this has relevance for the examples of application, it is not truly what was asked for. Emphasis is placed on following directions and sticking to the topic. These skills are forerunners of using thesis statements in paper writing.

*From Eugene Davis, *Electricity in Your Life* (Englewood Cliffs, N.J.: Prentice Hall, 1963).

Example 1:

The chemical effect of current isn't seen very much around your house. However, it is of great importance in industry. When an electric current is passed through some liquid chemical compounds, the current can break up the compounds into their separate elements. This process in called *electrolysis*.

Chlorine gas is manufactured by electrolysis. An electric current breaks down a solution of ordinary table salt, *sodium chloride,* into sodium and chlorine. The sodium combines with water to form a new compound, making the chlorine easy to collect.

The process is also used to obtain some of the raw materials for soaps, detergents, rayon, and many other products.

One of the most important uses of electrolysis is to separate aluminum from its ore. It takes 20,000 kilowatt-hours to make one ton of aluminum!

A variation of the electrolysis process is used to plate metals. Naturally enough, it is called *electroplating*. Chromium and nickel are commonly used as protective and decorative coatings on iron and steel. Silver and gold are often used to plate jewelry made of cheap metal. You know that we can't *see* electricity. We can only see the *effect* it has. The four effects of electric current are *thermal* (heat giving), *luminous* (light giving), *chemical* (causing chemical changes), and *magnetic* (creating magnetism).

All of these effects depend on changing the electrical energy to some other form. To a scientist, energy means *the ability to do work*. Energy is never lost but it can be changed from one form to another.

When electricity flows through a poor conductor, not much of the current gets through. What happens to the energy? It is changed to heat.

All electrical appliances that use heating elements are really using wires that are poor conductors. The most common wire used for this purpose is *nichrome,* an alloy.

Electric heaters, ranges, ovens, irons, toasters, soldering irons, clothes dryers, and hair dryers, all depend on the thermal, or heating, effect of current.

The luminous effect of current is one which you see constantly—every time you turn on an electric light. If both the current and the resistance in a conductor are very high, the conductor gets so hot that it glows. The nichrome wires in a heating element glow, but not enough to read by. The wire in an ordinary light bulb is a special type of wire that glows brightly and doesn't burn out. Other types of lighting depend on making a gas or chemical glow by passing a current through it. Neon and fluorescent lights are examples of these types.

The magnetic effect of current is one which plays a big part in your everyday life. It makes your telephone, doorbell, and tape recorder work, and it helps you send a telegram.

Whenever current flows through a wire, the area around the wire becomes magnetic and is called a *magnetic field*. This fact was discovered in 1819 by the Danish physicist and chemist, Hans Christian Oersted.

You have probably played with a bar or horseshoe magnet that picks up nails, pins and other iron objects. This is a *permanent magnet* because it is magnetic all the time.

If you place a core of iron inside a coil of wire and pass a current through the wire, the iron and the coil together become a magnet. This is called an *electromagnet*. As soon as you turn off the current, the electromagnet is not a magnet any more. We say that an electromagnet is a *temporary magnet*.

Electromagnets on cranes are often used in factories or in auto junkyards to lift heavy weights of steel. With the current on, the magnet holds fast to a huge load of metal while the crane lifts it and swings it into place. As soon as the current is switched off, the magnetism stops and the steel is unloaded.

A much smaller electromagnet makes an electric bell ring. The magnet attracts a part of the bell called the *armature*. When the armature is pulled toward the magnet the circuit is broken. Immediately, the current shuts off and the armature drops back. But as soon is it drops, the current flows again and the armature is quickly pulled back to the electromagnet. And so it goes, back and forth, back and forth. A little hammer on the end of the armature strikes against a gong each time—and it is that steady ding, ding, ding in very rapid succession that makes the sound of a ringing bell.

Organizing Notes

Before a rough draft can be written, some type of sequencing or organizing of the notes taken must occur. There are several ways to provide practice in organizing information. The student must learn to identify relationships among facts. At the most basic level a student may have five facts related to a topic such as an animal. They need to recognize subtopics and group facts according to these subtopics. For example, facts about the animal's food, shelter, and physical description comprise different subtopics. When writing their rough drafts, students need to learn to include all information on one subtopic before introducing another subtopic.

A note sheet in the form of a puzzle can help with this concept (see Fig. 2). Students take down their facts, one per puzzle piece, just as they come to them. The students then number these facts in the order in which they will use them in their written paragraph. Then the teacher has a conference with the student to check the accuracy of the work. It is quite possible that an important part of a fact has been omitted. For example, something about the sound a seahorse makes should be added to the seventh puzzle piece on the Seahorse note sheet. The seahorse makes a *clicking* sound when it snaps its neck. The beginning student will need this kind of teacher supervision and assistance.

The next level of sophistication is sequencing the subtopics in a logical order. For example, start with the physical description; follow with food, shelter, defenses; then life cycle.

At this point it is appropriate to have students focus on structural relationships such as general to specific, or parts to a whole.

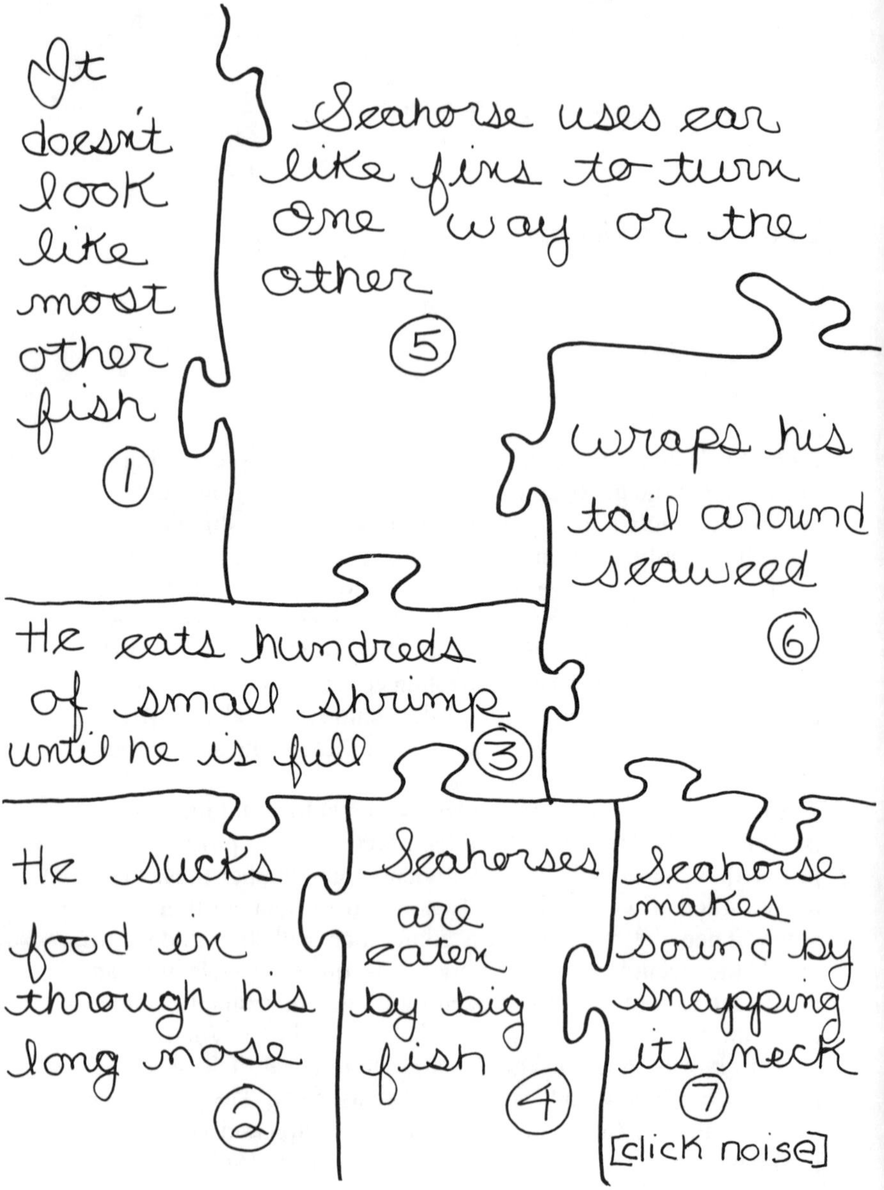

Puzzle pieces:

1. It doesn't look like most other fish ①
2. He sucks food in through his long nose ②
3. He eats hundreds of small shrimp until he is full ③
4. Seahorses are eaten by big fish ④
5. Seahorse uses ear like fins to turn one way or the other ⑤
6. wraps his tail around seaweed ⑥
7. Seahorse makes sound by snapping its neck ⑦ [click noise]

FIG. 2

Other relationships such as, cause and effect, comparing and contrasting, categorizing, and the use of symbolism, also help provide organizational schemes for sequencing notes prior to draft writing.

OUTLINING

Among the strategies for organizing notes, outlining is probably the most common. Students are taught that if there is a *I*, there must be a *II*; if there is an *A*, there must be a *B*. If something is divided into parts there must be more than one part. Otherwise there is no need for division. Outlining emphasizes the general to specific relationship among facts, and usually is an appropriate approach.

Exercises that provide practice in relating the whole to its parts (the general to the specific) can be created on any topic. In the beginning, it is best to provide both the outline format and the words which will be used to fill in the blanks. Later, just the list of words is enough. At that stage of development, there may easily be more than one "right" outline sequence, and class discussions regarding alternate possibilities are fruitful uses of class time.

Outlining Exercise 1

Words to use: Beef, Cheese, Corn, Food, Ice cream, Meat, Milk, Peas, Pork, Vegetables

Topic
  I.
    A.
    B.
  II.
    A.
    B.
  III.
    A.
    B.

Outlining Exercise 2

Words to use: Ball-and-socket, Elbow, Hinge, Hip, Joints, Knee, Knuckle, Shoulder

Topic
I.
   A.
   B.
II.
   A.
   B.
   C.

Outlining Exercise 3

Words to use: Areas, Bay, Dolphin, Fish, Fresh, Frog, Inhabitants, Lake, Mussel, Ocean, Oyster, Pond, River, Salt, Sea, Seaweed, Water, Whales

Just as in the previous exercise, *A* and *B* could be reversed, other variations become acceptable. In this exercise, the terms Areas and Inhabitants would be used twice, and the 1, 2, and 3 divisions would be further subdivided using *a,b,* and *c,* etc. It is important that students begin to develop their own outline formats and not depend on given formats to help them to determine levels of relationships.

A concept regarding outlining that is sometimes missed is that an outline works when information is known and it works when information is not known. Known facts can be organized using an outlining format, or an organizational outline can be created to be used as a guide for locating as yet unknown facts. With young students it is usually more effective to give them an outline to work from. When the teacher develops the outline based on materials in the collection, the teacher's main points are sure to be covered and there is a guarantee that the material is available to the students. As student skill increases and overall ability in search technique is developed, it becomes reasonable to expect students to develop presearch outlines. A transition into student-developed outlines could be to have students structure outlines for the plot of a narrative creative assignment. This provides practice in structuring ideas without having also to use search skills.

WEBBING

Sometimes a less formal structure is easier to work with. Webbing is one of these. (See Fig. 3 for an example of a web.) Its

SAMPLE OF A WEB:

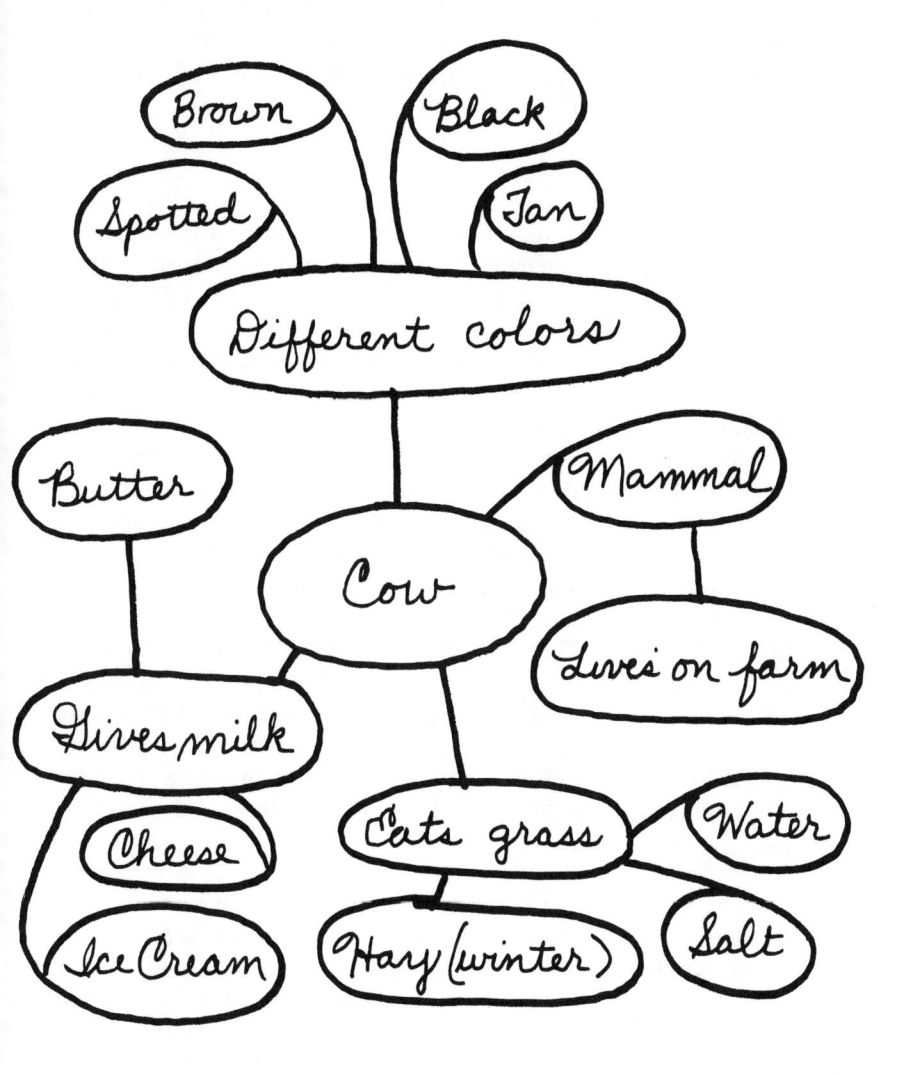

FIG. 3

The value of using a web to organize ideas is that additions can be made without having to rewrite the entire device as is the case with an outline.

advantages are that it shows multiple interrelationships, is visually concrete, and may be revised without rewriting. Webs may be used to analyze as well as to create structure. Comprehension of narrative plot and character traits can be illustrated through a web, just as webbed facts can be woven into a story.

FLOWCHARTING

Similarly, flowcharting can be used to analyze and create structure. Although flowcharting is more applicable to narration than exposition, a student may need to do some research to make a story authentic. The advantage of a flowchart is that it provides a means of identifying decision-making points within the story. As with webbing or outlining, it can be used to precede writing or to demonstrate comprehension.

An example of the application of flowcharting to show comprehension is provided in the following pages. A story dictated by second graders is used. The introductory pages of a juvenile novel were read to the entire class as a part of a library visit, and the children were asked to write the continuation of the story themselves. The class "brainstormed" a variety of directions the story might take. They took a vote and chose their favorite. A committee of "writers" were sent back to the library media center at a later time to work with the school library media teacher and the software program, *Bank Street Writer*. They created a story which was later presented to the class for reactions. The story and flowchart (see Fig. 4) follow.

"Tyro in Space"

Tyro was outside the spaceship fixing the space camera when the ship took off. They forgot Tyro was outside and he fell off the spaceship. He fell deep in space. He felt lonely and afraid. He fell into a deep sleep. When he woke up he felt thirsty and hungry. He didn't have a lunchbox with him, but he had a Milky Way candybar and a Star Cookie. He ate the Star Cookie and saved the candybar for later because he didn't know how long he would be floating in space.

Back on Earth they were getting ready to launch the space shuttle Discovery. Buck Rogers was the captain. He was in charge of a crew of eight. Four of them were women and four were men. Their job was to bring back a satellite to Earth.

When they got to the satellite they saw a green subject with antennas sitting on the satellite. Buck Rogers was curious. He ordered the arm of the shuttle to take the satellite and Tyro in. They closed the bay doors and the crew went to look at what they had brought in. Tyro scrunched up against the satellite to hide. He was scared. The Earth people asked him his name. When he answered it sounded like music. Tyro thought he had been captured by enemies. To make friends he took out his Milky Way candybar and offered to share it.

The Earth people taught him to speak Earth language. Tyro taught them to speak his language. They made contact with his ship and they came back for Tyro. Tyro was excited to be going home. He was also kind of sad. He had to leave his new friends behind. The captain of Tyro's ship promised to come back and visit the next time they were in the solar system.

FIG. 4

FLOWCHART FOR "TYRO IN SPACE" GROUP WRITING, "BRAINSTORMING" SESSION

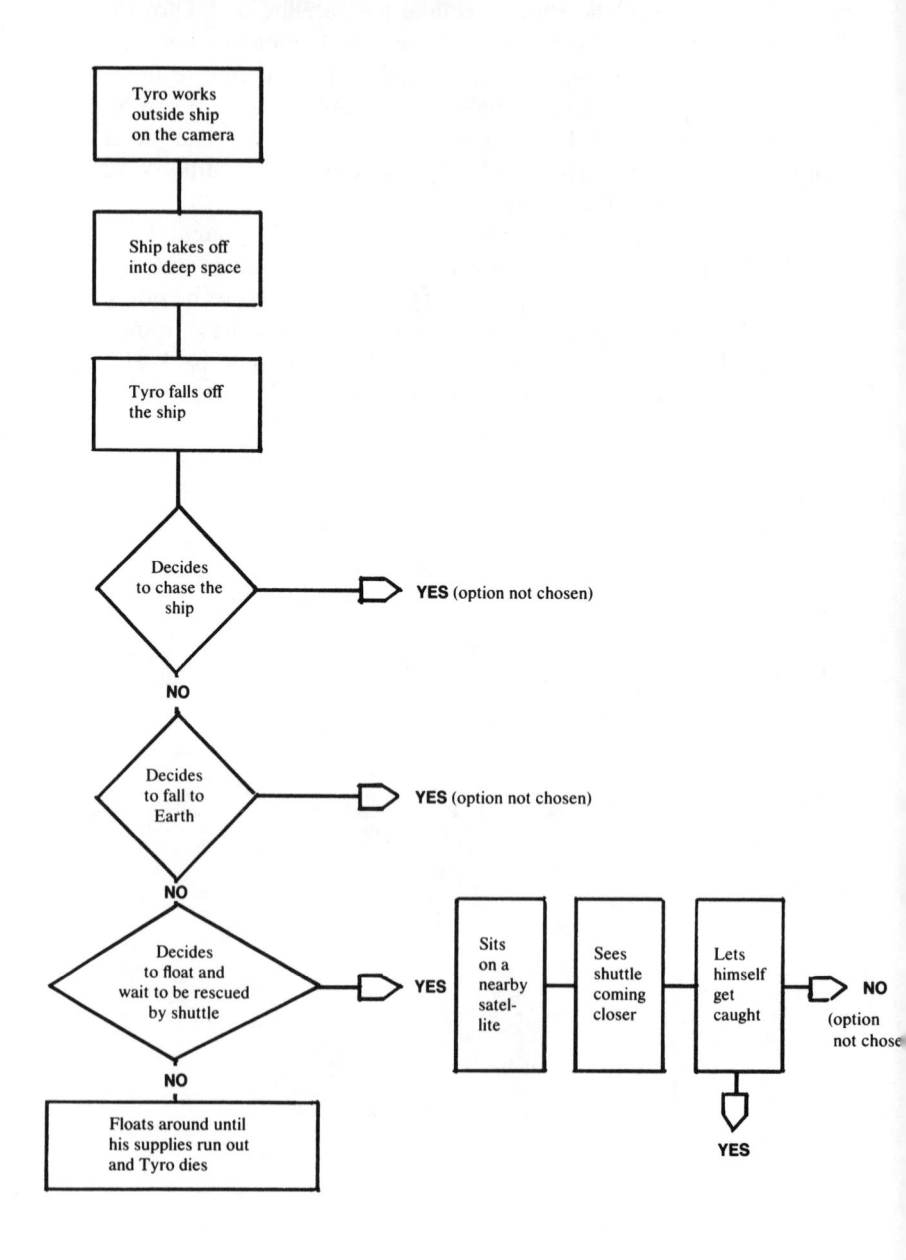

- Tyro works outside ship on the camera
- Ship takes off into deep space
- Tyro falls off the ship
- Decides to chase the ship — **YES** (option not chosen) / **NO**
- Decides to fall to Earth — **YES** (option not chosen) / **NO**
- Decides to float and wait to be rescued by shuttle — **YES** → Sits on a nearby satellite → Sees shuttle coming closer → Lets himself get caught → **NO** (option not chosen) / **YES**
- **NO** → Floats around until his supplies run out and Tyro dies

YES

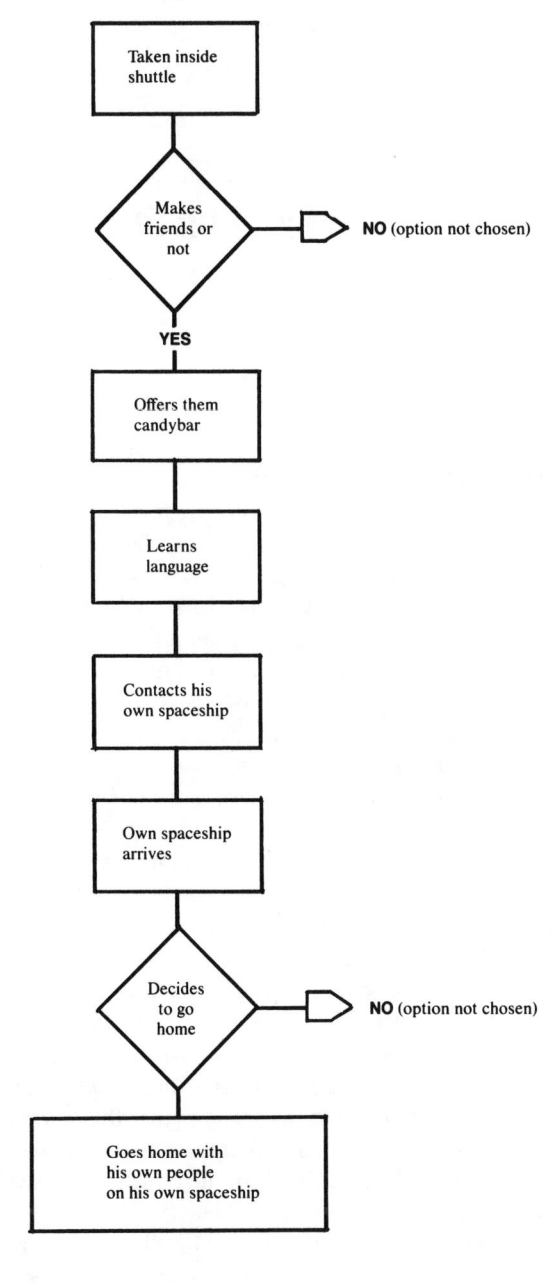

```
┌──────────────┐
│   Taken inside│
│   shuttle    │
└──────┬───────┘
       │
      ◇ Makes friends or not ──→ ▷ **NO** (option not chosen)
       │
     **YES**
       │
┌──────┴───────┐
│  Offers them │
│  candybar    │
└──────┬───────┘
┌──────┴───────┐
│   Learns     │
│   language   │
└──────┬───────┘
┌──────┴───────┐
│ Contacts his │
│ own spaceship│
└──────┬───────┘
┌──────┴───────┐
│ Own spaceship│
│   arrives    │
└──────┬───────┘
       │
      ◇ Decides to go home ──→ ▷ **NO** (option not chosen)
       │
┌──────┴──────────────┐
│ Goes home with      │
│ his own people      │
│ on his own spaceship│
└─────────────────────┘
```

Revision In The Writing Process

Working from a "barking" draft (which is rough, rough), one begins the three-stage writing process of revising, editing, and proofreading. During the revision process, the student concentrates on improving the content, clarity, and organization of information. At this stage of the process, the student is not concerned with mechanical errors including spelling, punctuation, and grammar. These will be addressed later. The ideas are the important component at the onset. The ideas must be put down before they can be polished.

The second stage, editing, concentrates on improving sentence structure, paragraph structure, and vocabulary. The mechanical skills are still "on hold." There is no harm in making a mechanical correction when it is observed, but the thrust of this part of the process is on vocabulary development and style of sentence structure. Sentence fragments, run-on sentences, and overused expressions are replaced with more appropriate wording.

The third stage, proofreading, emphasizes the mechanics. Now is the time to verify spellings, punctuation, capitalization, and other refinements. The ideas have been expressed, the organization is sound, so attention can be turned to mechanics. The advantage of this sequence is that ideas take priority over technical aspects. Once the ideas are in place, the rewriting can happen, whereas the reverse, placing emphasis on mechanics at too early a stage, will stifle the ideas and discourage the students.

The following three drafts show the results of emphasizing the writing process stage by stage. The "barking" draft reappears as a revised draft; the revised draft becomes the edited draft which would become the final draft once spelling, punctuation, and capitalization had been proofread and corrected. The final draft is not shown.

SAMPLE DRAFTS FOR REVISION WRITING EXERCISE:
Barking Draft: (Rough, Rough!)

Holloween is my favorite holiday.
When I was a child I didn't get to go thick or treating.
I like Halloween stuff. My mother never let me chew gumm.
We lived out in the country with no close naybors.
They have too be very carful now.
People put things in apples and candy.
It is dangerous holiday for kids.
They could get hitted by a cars.
They're costumnes can catched on fire and birn.
It is safer to go to a party then to go trick or treating.
I would have one a prise for my broom costume at a school party
only I didn't stay in the middle of the circle and then they
couldn't fine me again and then I didn't get the prise.

Revised Draft: Content, Clarity, and Organization Improved

Holloween is my favorite holiday.

I like Halloween stuff. We lived out in the country with no close naybors. When I was a child I didn't get to go thick or treating. We had a Halloween party at school each year. I would have one a prise for my broom costume at a school party only I didn't stay in the middle of the circle and then they couldn't fine me and then I didn't get a prise.

Kids have to be very carful now. Halloween is very dangerous because people put things in apples and candy. They can get hitted by a cars. There costumnes can catched on fire and birn. It is safer to go to a party than trick or treating.

Edited Draft: Edited for Sentence Structure and Vocabulary Improvement

Holloween is my favorite holiday because I like the candy and gumm you can get. My family and I lived out in the country with no close naybors When I was a child I didn't get to go trick or treating. The town sponsored an annual Halloween party at the elementary school. One year I wrote an unusual cosume. I swept the judges off there feet with my realistic broom outfit. The judges selected me as a prise winner and escorted me to the center of the circle In as much as they did not explain to me why I was singled out I wandered back into the crowd of witches ghosts gobblins hobos clowns and other asorted characters. The judges slected an alternate individual to receive the prise as they could not find me a second time.

Today kids have to be very carfull when they go thick or treating. Holloween has become very dangerious because some crazy people put items such as pins needles razor blades or drugs in the Halloween candy or apples. Because of increased traffic youngsters have to be alert when crossing streets. Many store bought costumes could be a fire hazzard as well. Due to changes in society it has become safer to attend a nayborhood party than to go trick or treating house to house.

Students are more able to recognize structural deficiencies in other people's writing than in their own. Omissions in unfamiliar writing samples are more evident to them. One good way to introduce students to the stages of the writing process is to present a sample to the whole class and demonstrate the process with them. These demonstrations should be conducted at each step of the process, and should be repeated until the students can begin to implement the process on their own. These teacher/student demonstrations lead naturally into the use of peer conferencing to improve writing.

Peer Conferencing

Peer conferencing is a method that accomplishes at least two things. The students gain skill in analyzing and revising written passages, and the classroom teacher is saved considerable time by not grading initial drafts. There are variations in the ways peer conferences are structured. There can be a pair of students reacting to each other's writing, or there can be a committee working on related topics and interacting with each other. In either case the student author shares a written passage with peers who make suggestions for improvements. The student author then revises the passage and the process is repeated as often as necessary to meet peer group expectations. This draft is then shared with the classroom teacher for final conference editing. The paper is rewritten once more and turned in for grade.

Students cannot do successful peer conferencing without instruction and practice. A good initiating activity is to begin with a sentence-length passage such as "The notebook is in the desk." One student assumes the role of author and writes the sentence down. The second student becomes the questioner. The questioner begins by saying something positive about the author's work. At this level it may be as irrelevant as, "I like the color ink you use.", or "You spelled every word right." The point is to begin the peer conference with some positive interaction.

The next phase of the conference is to have the questioner ask questions about things that are unclear. For example, "What color is the notebook?", "What do you use it for?", "What is the desk made out of?", and "Where is the desk?" The author jots these questions down and then rewrites the sentence to incorporate answers to these questions. The resulting sentence might be expanded to, "The red spiral notebook I use for science class is in the bottom drawer of the white desk in my bedroom."

Follow-up sessions would include passages such as the following examples describing a teacher's desk and a backyard fish pond. When using paragraph length examples (or longer ones), the point is to encourage higher order level questions. For example, instead of asking how many drawers the desk has, the goal is to elicit questions such as, "How do you feel when working at the desk?"

SAMPLE PARAGRAPHS FOR PEER CONFERENCE PRACTICE (WHOLE CLASS)

1. I have a desk at home.
   It is large and has many drawers.
   On one side is a typewriter and on the other side is a lamp.
   It is covered with papers.
   I plan lessons and create activities there.

2. My backyard has a pond.
   A number of different things live in it.
   There is a garden beside the pond.
   Around the edge of the yard is a fence.
   I like being in my yard.

One method of presentation is to project a transparency of the passage. The teacher reads it sentence by sentence. The students ask questions that come to their minds about each sentence such as, things they want to know more about, things that are unclear, etc. The teacher jots these ideas down around the edge of the passage and makes revisions by writing on the transparency. Students observe some revision techniques like insertion, deletion, and moving words and sentences. They observe how the "messy" stages of rewriting work.

The next stage is to have students write their own material and procede in a similar manner to improve their own writing. There are numerous variations that may be used. For example, the following assignment was given to a class that was studying the concepts of rotation and revolution of planets: "In your group, decide on the speed of rotation, the cycle of revolution, and the shape of an orbit. Incorporate these facts into a story by describing life on your planet." Original drafts tended to use statements to tell the length of day and year rather than to describe events that would allow the reader to infer this information. The drafts were reproduced on transparencies and shared with the class during a discussion session. An example of what was hoped for, created by the teacher, was also shared. (Teacher's samples follow students' samples below.) Students were sent back to create new drafts with a better understanding of the assignment. These drafts were revised by using the writing process outlined above. Samples of initial drafts from this assignment follow.

SAMPLES OF UNCORRECTED STUDENT WORK: ROTATION AND REVOLUTION STORIES

1. Uniron is a small planet. The form of life on Uniron is the unicorn. One day Enie was flying on his cloud and he threw rocks out of the window at the evil apple. The evil apple eats unicorns for energy so he can rule the world. Enie got help from the wise unicorn. The wise old unicorn said, "I will give you a potion to ward off the evil apple." Enie made an announcement and put the potion on all the unicorns. The evil apple sent his worrier worms to get a unicorn because he was starting to rot . . . (end of time)

    (Note: This has good potential for a story line, but missed the point of the assignment.)

2. Here on the planet Iltaristruckt people live a happy life because it is spring all year long. Because our orbit is an equal diamond shape around the sun. TC woke up on the first morning of Junawoona and said, "HO hum another day another 70 hrs." Meanwhile DA was finishing his third breakfast of the day. Then he went to his computer room and started learning Senior Algebra. While TC was in bed he called his dog to fetch his Starstruck Times Newspaper . . .

    (Note: Here we have a couple of sentences that are on target—three breakfasts a day infers long day, however saying "seventy hours" has to go because directions asked for inferred information rather than specific statistics.)

3. About ten yrs ago we crashed on the planet Palms. Ever since then we have noticed that the day consists of 12 hrs. and there are only 180 days in a yr. The temperature is usually in the 70's

and they only have one enemy, the BEGAL. Which is a mixture of a bat and an eagle. Now that we have been here we have different jobs and hobbies. Which are fishing, bird watching, swimming and surffing. We don't have to fish that often because there are only two meals a day—brunch and dinner.

(Note: Here we have some good sentences to infer from, particularly the one about new jobs and hobbies. The earlier sentence about observing the day and year have potential, but went astray by saying the length outright.)

4. We are superior beings. We live in indestructable silicone houses because of the abrupt turn that happens every 1.950 days. This happens because of our triangular orbit. Vega is our sun and Vega-Vega is our moon. We have to wear sunglasses at night because Vega-Vega is so bright.

(Note: Again, good story potential and a hint of what was wanted.)

TEACHER-CREATED SAMPLES

1. The alarm went off. I didn't want to get up. It seemed as though I had just laid my head down on my pillow. I had snuggled under the covers and gone right to sleep. It seemed too early for the alarm to be ringing. I don't do well unless I get a full night's sleep. Occasionally I can function on 120 minutes of sleep a night, but I do much better with a full 210 minutes of sleep.

(Note: Because 210 minutes equals a full night's sleep, a short rotation period is inferred—shorter than an Earth night.)

2. My favorite holiday is Samtirsrch. As I remember, this holiday was fun because we got presents and ate special foods. I don't really remember Samtirsch last year, but my parents tell me how much fun I had and how cute I looked in my red fuzzy sleeper. Looking at the family pictures I can't believe how small I was just last year.

(Note: Poor memory of holiday last year infers long revolution—much longer than an Earth year.)

Checklist

An aid to both the teacher and student in preparing written assignments is the use of a checklist. As students work through the process, they are guided step by step, and are also able to avoid omissions. By using the evaluative criteria listed, they are able to evaluate their own work. The teacher's expectations are spelled out in the checklist. This is a help to parents who wish to acquaint themselves with their child's assignments, and it is also a written record of expectations. Receiving this checklist at the beginning of the assignment helps reduce misunderstandings as the assignment progresses. Another advantage of using a checklist of this sort is that it reduces the subjectivity of grading. Fairness is built in.

The checklist is useful even when the teacher chooses to do just one part of the process, or chooses to weight various parts of the process differently because of the emphasis of the current assignment. In the first instance, the students see where the part they are doing fits into the whole. In the second instance, each part may equal fifteen percent of the total grade which would equal ninety points and be an A grade. The remaining ten percent allows for teacher judgment to reward effort, improvement, aesthetics, or other embellishments. If the teacher wishes to weight the various parts differently, giving more value to note cards than selection of topic or sources, adjusting the percentages assigned each section accordingly takes care of the problems. Percentages are easily changed from assignment to assignment. The checklist becomes a grading sheet as well as a learning tool.

PROJECT WRITING CHECKLIST

Your topic: _____ Name: _____

		YES	NO
I.	Topic		
	A. Is your topic broad enough?	___	___
	B. Is your topic narrow enough?	___	___
	C. Is your topic approved by the teacher?	___	___
	D. Is your topic of interest to you?	___	___
II.	Note Cards		
	A. Are you writing only key words and phrases?	___	___
	B. Is the information on each card related to only one question?	___	___
	C. Is the information on each card from only one source?	___	___
	D. Are your cards labeled with the question #?	___	___
	E. Are your cards labeled with the source #?	___	___
	F. Is information related to all questions included?	___	___
	G. Is a bibliography card included for each source?	___	___
III.	Sources		
	A. Have you included information from at least three sources?	___	___
	B. Have you used different kinds of sources?		
	1. General encyclopedia	___	___
	2. Trade book	___	___
	3. A.V. materials	___	___
	4. Specialized reference books	___	___
	5. Periodical or newspaper	___	___
IV.	Organization		
	A. Have you put your note cards into groups related to each of your questions?	___	___
	B. Have you arranged the cards in order within each group?	___	___
	C. Have you met with peer group members and shared your organizational structure?	___	___
	D. Have you made changes according to their suggestions for improvement?	___	___

V. Rough Draft
   A. Did you write it from your note cards?   ___ ___
   B. Did you include a paragraph of
      introduction?   ___ ___
   C. Did you include at least one paragraph for
      each question?   ___ ___
   D. Does it make sense when you read it?   ___ ___
   E. Have you made a sketch of any illustrations
      to be included?   ___ ___
   F. Have you shared your draft with the
      members of your group?   ___ ___
   G. Have you made any changes suggested by
      the group?   ___ ___
   H. Have you met with your teacher to verify:
      1. Spelling   ___ ___
      2. Capitalization   ___ ___
      3. Punctuation   ___ ___
      4. Grammar   ___ ___
      5. Paragraph placement   ___ ___

VI. Final Copy
   A. Is it neat?   ___ ___
   B. Is it accurate according to H above?   ___ ___
   C. Have you included a bibliography?   ___ ___
      1. Did you use correct form?   ___ ___
      2. Did you put your sources in ABC order?   ___ ___
   D. Did you include diagrams, charts, etc.?   ___ ___
      1. Are they neat?   ___ ___
      2. Do they communicate information
         clearly?   ___ ___

This checklist is intended to help you make sure you meet your teacher's expectations. If you follow through with each step in the process, you will have a successful finished product.

Another aspect of organizing information is being able to state a position and justify it. This is a desirable outcome of American education as it is a skill that is a basic requirement for an informed electorate. It is also an aspect of education not emphasized in the public education systems of other countries. It is not enough for our students to hear a lecture, take notes, and answer exams on the material mindlessly. Information needs to be analyzed, evaluated, and applied in some way. This process involves higher order learning skills.

To give opportunity to learn these skills, open ended situations with multiple defensible solutions need to be used. A further requirement is group interaction. These skills are difficult, if not impossible, to learn while working independently. One needs to respond to other peoples' ideas and see and hear their reactions to your ideas. It is the give and take that is crucial in developing these skills.

Providing this kind of practice for students is often discouraging to the teachers. Initial experiences can seem chaotic and a waste of time. However, it is only through repeated exposure that students fully develop these skills to the point where they will have them for life. Examples of ways to provide these experiences are addressed below in *Social Studies Enrichment Program*.

PART FOUR
SAMPLE RESEARCH PROJECTS

Curriculum-Related Activities

Once students have received instruction and been given practice opportunities related to the fundamental building block skills required to undertake a search project, they then need to move on into more demanding assignments that require the application of these skills. Having learned the process piecemeal, it is now time to put it all together. Assignments can and should be designed to incorporate all subject areas. Here is where it is important for teamwork between the school library media teacher and the classroom teacher to take place. It is also desirable to provide students with several shorter projects than to depend on a single major product. When search projects are evaluated on each part of the process as is done when the checklist approach is used, the sections in which a student is weaker than others can be identified and another attempt made. Gradually, the skill is learned. When only a single, annual project is assigned and a student does not do well with it, there is less chance of the student's learning the search processes.

The following activities all require research skills. They vary in terms of complexity, time commitment, and type of finished product. These activities can be used to differentiate instruction according to the ability of students. An entire class need not be assigned the same activity. These sample activities may be used as they are presented, or they may serve as models for adapting to local needs.

SHORT TERM PROJECTS

Beginners in information finding and paper writing need the opportunity to practice the skill repeatedly through short, fairly simple activities until they have mastered it. It cannot be emphasized enough that single questions provide practice in the search process.

The twelve activities that follow are all meant to be short term projects suitable for beginners' practice.

Dinosaurs

One topic that is of interest to many young students is dinosaurs. In an effort to introduce upper primary grade students to subheadings in the encyclopedia and to illustrate the difference between dictionaries and encyclopedias, the following activity was developed:

1. Write a definition for each of the following terms: *dinosaur, fossil,* and *extinct.*
2. Name the two kinds of dinosaurs. Tell how they are different. Give at least one example of each.
3. Make a list of ways in which the world changed during the Mesozoic Era.
4. Why did the dinosaurs die out? Do the experts agree?
5. As a group project, make a timeline showing when the dinosaurs lived. Each student will make an opaque enlargement of one kind of dinosaur. The picture will be labeled with the name of the dinosaur, its size, and when it lived. (This timeline can be displayed in the hall outside the students' classroom, in their classroom, or in the media center.)

These specific questions were developed to be used with the dinosaur article in *Worldbook Encyclopedia.* The topics match the subheadings and use is made of the illustrations and timeline. An interesting aspect of working with dinosaur material is watching the students' reactions when they find discrepancies between sources. Some sources divide dinosaurs into three major kinds; others use two divisions and ascribe different characteristics to the categories. Interesting discussions can come out of such findings.

Shelters

Primary students can be introduced to the concept of shelter as something all living things need. After a discussion of the shelters they live in and see around them each student could be given a term for a specific type of shelter to investigate. Terms such as the following could be used:

1. *Apartment house*
2. *Igloo*
3. *Sampan*
4. *Tent*
5. *Castle*
6. *Mansion*
7. *Hotel*
8. *Dormitory*
9. *Cabin*
10. *Cave*

The end product of this research activity would be a class dictionary of terms for shelters around the world and throughout history. Each student would contribute a short entry describing the characteristics of their particular term. A picture could be included if desired. It would be advisable to check the availability of materials before assigning terms. A dictionary definition might be sufficient, but trade books on houses and shelters are available and can be helpful.

Rocks and Minerals

Rocks are of interest to many youngsters. In connection with a geology unit, a research activity might focus on different types of rocks. Each student could be assigned a specific type of rock to find out about. The final product could include the following:

1. Information about what the rock looks like.
2. Where it would most likely be found.
3. The minerals which comprise the rock type.
4. How it was formed.
5. Industrial uses of the minerals in the rock.
6. Any other interesting facts about the rock.

Simple Machines

Intermediate grade students studying simple machines could be asked to research a hand tool and explain the principles involved in its use. Once all simple machines had been introduced to the students, they could be asked to apply their new knowledge by identifying the simple machines involved in a particular tool's use, how the simple machines involved work, and how the relationship between force and distance is altered by using the tool. Examples of tools that could be used include:

1. Using a claw hammer to remove a nail. (Lever.)
2. Using a wheelbarrow to transport a load. (Lever and wheel and axle.)
3. Using a screwdriver to insert a screw. (Wheel and axle and screw.)
4. Using a pair of pliers to grip a nut. (Lever.)
5. Using a knife to cut an apple. (Wedge.)
6. Using a doorknob to open a door. (Wheel and axle.)
7. Using a hand-turned can opener to open a can. (Wedge and wheel and axle.)
8. Adjusting a wrench to size. (Screw.)
9. Using a chisel to cut away wood, stone, or metal, (Wedge.)
10. Using a vegetable peeler to skin a cucumber. (Wedge.)
11. Pushing the loaded wheelbarrow up a plank to a higher level. (Inclined plane.)
12. Using a crowbar to move a stone. (Lever.)

The end product could be a sales pitch giving the advantages of the tool in terms of the simple machine principles involved.

Human Body

Each student could be assigned an organ, type of joint, or other body part to investigate. Research would identify the following:

1. Location in the body.
2. Function.
3. Possible problems or diseases.
4. Physical description of the body part.

The finished products could be compiled into a booklet with the body parts organized into the major systems of the body. Appropriate illustrations could be included.

Chemical Elements

While chemistry is not studied in great depth in elementary science units, the concept that all matter is made up of a limited number of elements is presented. Students can be assigned an element to research in terms of the following:

1. How it was discovered.
2. Who discovered it.
3. Where it is found.
4. Its uses.

5. Its properties.
6. What it looks like.
7. Its symbol.

The finished product might be only a paragraph or two in length, but the research process would be practiced, and that is equally important "content" to be learned from this lesson.

Foods

In connection with a nutrition unit, have each student research a particular food. Students would discover where the food comes from, as in the following examples:

1. Meat—which animal.
2. Vegetable—which part of the plant.
3. Dairy products—sources.
4. How it is grown or raised.
5. Manufactured products, for example, both oil and hominy from corn.

The nutritional value could be included depending upon the concepts stressed in the unit of study. Once the information is shared with the class, a classification or webbing activity could follow and illustrate relationships between certain foods. For example, there could be a meat web, a vegetable and fruit web, or a web of products made from corn, or wheat, or peanuts, etc.

Inventions

Each student could be assigned an invention to research. Information to be found would include the following:

1. When it was invented.
2. Who invented it.
3. Why it was invented.
4. Its overall effect.

The final product could be an Invention Convention where each student plays the part of his or her inventor and tries to convince the class of the importance of a particular invention. Inventions could be ranked by the class from the one they believe has had the greatest impact on the world to the one with the least impact. Inventions could be confined to a particular period in history, such as the Industrial Revolution, or the list could include contributions from the ancient cultures through modern times. The students' reasons for the ranking would be an important component of the presentation of their inventions.

Sports

In an effort to capitalize on student interest in sports, research could be conducted on lesser known sports. Each student would be assigned a sport and asked to find the following information:

1. The rules of the sport.
2. Equipment needed.
3. Design of the playing field or court.
4. History and geographical areas where the sport is most often played.

During Olympic years, the lesser known Olympic sports would be a good starting point. Map skills could be practiced if a world map were coded with the geographic distribution information for each sport.

Natural Resources

Discuss a natural resource such as a tree, a cow, a peanut, petroleum or coal. Have the students brainstorm products which are derived from that resource. Have students research a product from their own lists of suggestions or one you add if the students are not able to produce a list to meet the class's needs. The final product might be a web that visualizes relationships among the products. Each student would have found information about the following.

1. The part of the resource used to produce the product.
2. The process used to produce the product.
3. How the product is used in daily life.

Once this information is shared, the class can construct the web.

Sound

Students could brainstorm topics of interest to them that are in some way related to the general topic of sound. Some topics might be related to the following:

1. Actual production of sound in musical instruments.
2. How sound is sent by telephone.

3. How sound is sent by satellite.
4. How sound is sent by TV.
5. How sonar and radar work.
6. Safety concerns related to noise pollution.
7. Relationship of speed of vibration to pitch.
8. Whatever else interests the students.

In small groups, students could generate a few questions to be answered about their chosen topic. Once the information is located and a draft is written, the group could meet and listen to each other's drafts and ask questions if something is not clear. A revision would be written and the finished segments could be compiled into a class booklet on the general topic of sound.

Clocks

When adjustments are made for daylight savings time, it might be interesting to have students research different methods of telling time. Included could be the following:

1. Different types of clocks—sundials to digitals.
2. Watches.
3. Time zones and their history.
4. Monuments such as Stonehenge.
5. Specific famous clocks such as Big Ben.
6. Clock makers such as Bannaker or Seth Thomas.

A discussion of why clocks have become more and more accurate over time, and what demands are made on modern day timepieces could serve as a conclusion to a mini unit on time.

MORE COMPLEX PROJECTS

As the student's skill improves the demands of the project must grow. One method is to structure several small segments of search that will be linked together to produce a larger, more complex product. The three activities that follow are examples that provide this next level of challenge.

Countries

Working from a common outline, each student could research a different country. They would look for the following information about each country:

1. Size, location, and physical features.
2. History and governmental system.
3. Resources and industries.
4. Customs and holidays.

Added features might include illustrations of the flag, a map, and any symbols of importance. By assigning one topic on the outline each week and requiring the students to turn in note cards, a rough draft, and the finished copy for that topic, the process will be practiced four times. Additionally, by breaking the project up into four small pieces, the students do not feel as intimadated by it. When the activity is structured in this way, neither the student nor the teacher is overwhelmed by the assignment. The grade is based upon all facets of the process and accumulates with each weekly segment. With slight adaptation this outline could be designed for use with states rather than countries.

Rivers

Students who are studying various regions of the earth or a number of world cultures could be asked to determine the most important river on each continent. In reaching their conclusions, it could be suggested that they consider the following:

1. River's vital statistics (length, size, volume of flow).
2. Uses (shipping, recreation, transportation).
3. Its involvement in historical events.

Once each student has prepared a case for making a particular choice, the results could be shared and graphed. After some discussion, a poll could be taken to determine whether the class is in agreement on the most important rivers.

Games

Discuss with your students what games they most enjoy playing. Have them think about why they enjoy those particular games and why certain others are at the bottom of their lists. Discuss the role of skill and luck in the playing of their favorite and most disliked games. Point out the need for balance between the two to make the game interesting. Discuss the various formats of games—board games, card games, manipulatives such as Cootie or Mousetrap, or simulations. Have each student, or a small group of students, select a game format and a topic to use in creating an educational game. Depending upon their interests they might select:

1. A time in history.
2. A math skill.
3. A reading skill.
4. A field of science.
5. An occupation.

Step one would be to locate sufficient facts about the topics to be able to design the game. Step two would be to produce a draft of the game (a game board and set of activity cards, or materials for a simulation) to be used by other students to see if it works. Are the directions clear? Is it fun to play? Is it at an appropriate difficulty level? Once it has been field-tested, the final game pieces can be constructed. If the pieces are well-made and attractive, these games pieces could be laminated and the games may become important instructional materials for your building.

MULTILEVEL ADAPTATIONS OF PROJECTS

The school library media center supplies many curricular topics and materials for student use. To make complete use of these, and to address the varying student ability levels within any given classroom or grade, multilevel applications must be developed. Three examples of research topics which can be adapted for use in primary, intermediate, and upper grade classrooms follow.

Animals

Primary students can be given an easy reading book about an individual animal. There are a number of these available on as low a reading level as the *I Can Read* books. After discussing with the students what a fact is, they can read their books and on a piece of paper divided into an appropriate number of sections, write one fact about the animal in each section. The next step is to confer with each student and together determine an appropriate sequence for the facts that have been chosen. This can be done by asking the student if any of the facts are about the same general topic, what the most interesting facts to start and end with are, and similar questions. The facts can then be numbered according to the student's answers, and written into a paragraph which becomes the final product.

Intermediate grade youngsters can be asked to read a nonfiction animal book for a book report. The final product might include the following:

1. A list of ten facts learned from reading the book.
2. A bibliographic entry using correct form.
3. Four clues to help classmates guess the identity of the animal.

Students are told to make the first two clues harder and the last two easier. It is best if the clues are written by the student and read to the class by the teacher. In this way, it is the strength of the clues, not students' interest in who read what book, that determines their answers. If individual students read their own clues, other students can answer based on knowing what animal that student was reading about.

Upper grade students can be asked to write a report on an assigned animal, working from a common outline and using a minimum of three sources. During week one of the project, the students take notes on the topics in Roman Numeral One of the following outline. They use these facts to write a rough draft and a finished copy for the information related to those topics only. During week two, the process is repeated for the topics in Roman Numeral Two, and so on until the outline topics are completed. The last week of the project is devoted to compiling the finished parts and adding a bibliography, table of contents, and a cover. In this way, the students have been through the research process a number of times and can practice the various steps—note taking, organizing the information, and polishing a draft. It is the mastery of this research *process* that is the ultimate goal of this type of instruction, not the specific facts about the topic which may or may not be retained.

The common outline might include the following topics:
I. Physical description
   A. Size and shape
   B. Surface covering
   C. Life cycle
II. Habitat
   A. Shelter
   B. Food
   C. Geographic distribution
III. Special features
   A. Defense

B. Enemies
   C. Adaptations
IV. Bibliography
   A. Animal book
   B. General encyclopedia
   C. Specialized reference

Biographical Research

Biographical sources provide a wide range of research activities. Primary students can be assigned a biography on their reading level and asked to write one sentence about the individual's childhood, one sentence about the person's adult life, and one sentence about the contributions made (or why this person is famous).

Intermediate grade students can be assigned a biography at their reading level and asked to take notes on the individual's early life, adult life, and contributions. Giving the student a page with puzzle pieces drawn on it can help motivate them. Each sheet is labeled with a topic and each puzzle piece is filled in with one fact related to that topic.

Part two of the assignment is to sequence the facts from the puzzle sheets into a sentence outline.

Part three is to have the students write a three paragraph report on their individual, using the sentence outline and adding the necessary transition words and sentences to make the report flow.

A cover could be added if desired, and a bibliographic entry for the book could be required. This assignment would be given after instruction in note taking and outlining had been presented. The final grade should take into consideration the notes, the outline, and the finished report.

Upper grade students could be expected to use a variety of biographical resources. The focus of this activity is biography as a form of literature.

Part 1:

1. Define biography as a literary form.
2. Compare and contrast biographies with autobiographies.
3. Define contemporary. (Alive at the same time—not necessarily modern.)
4. Define biographical dictionary as a specialized dictionary in

which paragraph-length entries are biographies rather than definitions of words. Examples: *Webster's New Biographical Dictionary* or *Who's Who in America*.
5. Look up the following people in a biographical dictionary and tell in one sentence what they are remembered for: Marcus Daly, William Harvey, Robert Lovett, John Muir, William Schuman, and Carl Sandburg.
6. Write a one-page autobiography.

Part 2:

1. Read the biography assigned to you for this project. (The reason for assigning is so students will read about an individual they do not already know a lot about and to avoid duplication.)
2. Write a report that includes information about your person's early life, education, career, accomplishments, and at least three of the person's contemporaries. Include a bibliography (minimum of three sources).
3. Share your information orally with the class.

Part 3:

1. Classify the individuals studied in as many ways as possible. For example, career fields, life spans, homelands.
2. Compile a mini biographical dictionary. Each student prepares an entry for their assigned individual. (This can be done with 4" × 6" or 5" × 7" index cards and a file box.)

A scavenger hunt could be prepared that would require the students to use all the biographical references in your collection. Questions would need to be worded in such a way as to give a hint as to the most appropriate source to use. For example, if your collection includes *Something About the Author,* the question might be stated as, "Steven Kellogg is the author of what books?" In this way, the student would know to choose a biographical reference which contains authors. If you have *Current Biography* a question might ask about an individual who made newspaper headlines during a particular year within your *Current Biography* holdings. The point is that the wording of the question needs to contain clues as to the career field, lifespan, or homeland of the individual so that the student can apply what they have learned about the organization of specialized reference tools.

Before an activity of this sort can be introduced successfully, the students must be given instruction related to the specific biographical references included in your collection. The type of individual included in the book, its arrangement, any unusual abbreviations, etc. must be covered. When developing an answer sheet, it is best to include space for the student to indicate the book and page where answers were found. This will save time in tracking down divergent answers.

Black History

Many school systems emphasize the contributions of Blacks during February. This provides a natural opportunity for integrating research.

As a class group, the students could produce an alphabet of famous Blacks. Each student could have a letter of the alphabet and make a poster showing the individual, state what the major accomplishments were, and prepare a label including individual's name and birth and death dates.

Create a chronological listing (timeline) of individuals alive during a specific period of time, such as the industrial revolution or the last twenty years.

Students could be given a list of names of famous Blacks and be asked to categorize them. In order to do this, the students would have to do some research to identify achievements, develop categories, and place the individuals in the appropriate categories.

Sources for identifying individuals for inclusion include the list of names at the end of the *Worldbook Encyclopedia* article, "Black Americans," index to *People Who Made America,* and collective biographies such as *Eight Black American Inventors*.

With Martin Luther King, Jr.'s birthday in effect as a national holiday, more and more schools will be developing celebration activities. The following questions were developed to allow second graders to find facts to use in writing about his life and death:

1. When and where was he born?
2. How did he get the name Martin?
3. Did he have any brothers or sisters?
4. What did his parents and grandparents do?
5. What schools did he go to?
6. Did he get married and have children?

7. Whose teachings impressed him?
8. What was his main goal?
9. How did he try to achieve his goal?
10. What award did he get in 1957?
11. What award did he get in 1964?
12. Did everyone agree with his methods?
13. How was he treated?
14. How did he die?
15. What is written on his monument?

These questions were based upon the article about King in *Worldbook Encyclopedia* and *Compton's Encyclopedia*. When a group of students came to work in the school library media center, they were given the appropriate volumes from both sets and were asked to look for the answers to the questions. They filled in the facts on a communal sheet. This was then used to write a group report. Answering the questions as they are sequenced assured that the structure for their report was built in. At this level such structure is crucial. After a number of experiences with teacher-structured activities, the students can begin to create the structure for themselves.

A REGULARLY SCHEDULED, INTEGRATED, RESEARCH-BASED DISCUSSION PROGRAM

If the search process and thought practice are to become important in school curriculum, it will be necessary to provide well-developed programs such as the Social Studies Enrichment Program (STEP). The acronym is slightly inaccurate, but the teachers' consensus was that *STEP* sounded better than *SSEP*, and that there is nothing really wrong with using the *ST* from *studies*. The STEP program, which is described in the following section, is an example of a staff-initiated project that incorporates research and higher order thinking skills into the curriculum on a regularly-planned, weekly basis. Although it was developed as part of the social studies program, its format could be transferred to other content areas.

The program was developed in response to the concerns expressed by parents of gifted students who were seeking additional academic challenge for their children. As it turns out, all students can benefit from this program which addresses the needs of each student.

Social Studies Enrichment Program (STEP)

STEP is a social studies enrichment program developed to provide differentiated instruction for students of various levels of ability. One day a week, during their social studies time, the students at a given grade level are regrouped according to ability. The most able students from each social studies class are pulled together in one room to interact with an open-ended question of the week. The questions are designed so that the students must apply the information that is being addressed during regular social studies class meetings. Using the facts presented by their regular teacher, the text, or other source materials, the students are asked to predict, evaluate, or make decisions as if they were living in the period being studied. For the first twenty or thirty minutes they discuss their positions and give their reasons for them. At the conclusion of the discussion each student writes a journal entry stating the problem, the facts related to it, and the personal position taken at the close of the discussion and why it was taken. The final few minutes of the period are spent introducing and clarifying the question for the following week because it is expected that these students will come to class prepared and ready to discuss the next issue. During the week they will have done any research necessary, talked the ideas over at home, and developed their position on the issue. Their positions may change as a result of the ideas presented during the discussion. The writing activity is intended to demonstrate the student's comprehension of the topic, as well as to improve writing skills.

The average and less able students are grouped together and given added practice on skills such as reading the text for the main idea and supporting details, note taking, and additional repetition of basic concepts related to the content being studied. Computer programs, films, and games are used to assure high interest while providing added practice of necessary skills.

The teachers at the given grade level decide which one of them will work with which group of students. It is possible to alternate semesters or even grading periods if teaching skill and style warrant it.

One needs to keep in mind that when initiating such a program it is unlikely that the first session will be totally successful. It takes practice to carry on a meaningful discussion. The idea that one's reason for a statement is as important, or even more important, than the statement itself is often a new concept to the students. These skills take time to become polished, but what better way to encourage thinking? The expository writing built into this program is different from the creative writing many students have been exposed to. Again, skills will improve with weekly practice.

The kinds of questions used are the key to the effectiveness of this program. Questions need to be open-ended, having no single correct answer, and be related to the on-going unit of study. In order to develop questions, the media specialist and the classroom teacher assigned responsibility for the top group sat down together with the curriculum guide and talked through the major points covered by the teacher. The questions were an outgrowth of this discussion. As the program has been implemented, there have been adjustments made in the pace which has caused teachers to skip some questions and to use two weeks on one question when necessary to develop the activity adequately. After the initial hesitations to be expected with any new program, STEP has become an integral part of this social studies program.

Sample fourth grade topic questions:

1. Regular class discussion will center on Maryland, where it is in the world, and in the United States. Attention is given to the geography of the state.

    QUESTION: Looking at an outline map of Maryland, how would you divide it into regions?

    Suggestions could be based upon physical geography, population, occupation, or use of land. The important point is to have the students justify the selected regional divisions in some way.

2. Regular class discussion (week 2) will center on the geography of Maryland. Attention is given to the great variations present within the state.

    QUESTION: Why is Maryland called America in miniature?

    Justification would include citing examples of various geographical features which exist within the state and comparing them to features of the United States as a whole.

3.–6. Regular class discussions (weeks 3 through 6) will focus on each of the major regions of the state. Emphasis will be on the geography and its impact upon occupations and daily life.

QUESTION: Where in the United States would you find similar conditions?
Attention would be given to climate, geography, occupations, etc.

7. Regular class discussions focus on the Delmarva (Delaware-Maryland-Virginia) Peninsula.
QUESTION: What services should be provided and what rules or regulations should be consistent for the total Delmarva Peninsula and which should be determined locally by the individual jurisdiction?
The emphasis is on justifying your answer.

Second marking period—History

1. Given what you know about the problems faced in seventeenth-century England and by the settlers in the New world, would you have chosen to stay in England or come to the new colony? Why?
2. Assess your household belongings. Decide what you would bring with you if you emigrated and what you would do with belongings you had to leave behind.
3. Are there any similarities in the relationships between the Native Americans and the early settlers and the present day relationship between industrial and developing nations?
Points to consider: sharing of technology, supplies, and ideas.
4. Throughout history, different cities have served as the capitol of the United States. What qualities are needed to make a good capitol city? Did the cities used throughout history meet them? What city would be the best choice now?
5. You are in charge of planning a new colony on an offshore island. Identify how you would provide the necessary services for the two hundred settlers.
Attention should be directed toward government, shelter, food, and protection.
6. Given a list of ten famous Marylanders, rank them according to their importance. Justify your ranking.
7. Compare self-sufficiency as demonstrated by the manor/plantation system with interdependency as illustrated by your daily life.
8. Create a list of historical sites that would be appropriate for field trips. Justify your choices.

Fifth Grade Topic Questions

1. If you were a Native American living in North America before the settlers arrived, would you rather have been a member of the Iroquois or Piscataway tribe? Why?
2. How would your life be different if you were a member of a tribe that got most of its food by farming or of a tribe which got most of its food by hunting?
3. Compare and contrast the governmental structure of the Iroquois Nation with our United States government.
4. What evidence of Indian culture and/or daily life is still around today?
5. If you were a reigning king or queen and an explorer came to you asking for financial support for explorations, what information would you want to know before saying yes or no?
6. Why did exploration occur to such a great extent during the 1400s and 1500s? Why not earlier or later?
7. Rank the following explorers in terms of the impact or importance of their discovery: Balboa, DeSota, Drake, Hudson, and Magellan. Explain your ranking.

Second marking period

1. Given the choice would you have stayed in Europe or come to settle in a new colony?
2. Compare and contrast successful and unsuccessful colonies. What made the difference?
3. Lifestyles in the New England, Mid-Atlantic, and Southern colonies were very different. What were these differences and what factors led to them?
4. In order to make a country work as a unit, what rules and services should be uniform and which could better be handled regionally?
5. If you had been a delegate to the Continental Congress, would you have signed the Declaration of Independence?
6. Taxes created discontent for the colonist as they still do today. Which type of tax were the colonists most upset about? (Stamp, tea, sugar, etc.) What present-day type of tax are people most upset about? (income, sales, property, etc.)
7. Explain how a fledgling nation could beat a world power as happened in the American Revolution.
8. Rank these individuals according to the importance of their

contributions: Adams, Franklin, Hancock, Jefferson, and Washington. Justify your ranking.
9. Different cities have served as the capitol of the United States. What qualities are needed to make a good capitol city? Did the cities used meet the criteria? (This question is similar to the one used in fourth grade because curriculum in the two grades overlap. Fourth grade curriculum includes Annapolis which was an early capitol city. Fifth grade studies colonial America, which includes early U.S. capitol cities.)

Sixth Grade Topic Questions

Egypt

1. Apparently, a major new archeological find has been discovered. It is authentic or not? What processes would you use to determine its authenticity?
2. What factors would an Egyptian home builder need to consider when choosing where to build the family's home?
3. It was customary to be buried with possessions in order to insure the quality of one's afterlife. If it were still the custom, what would you select to take with you now?
4. Rank the following technological innovations in terms of their importance to later civilizations: waterwheel, lintel and post, irrigation, calendar, sailing ships, and hieroglyphics.
5. If you were living in Egypt in ancient times, which of the following occupations would you choose? Potter, scribe, priest, slave, trader, farmer, or king. Why?
6. When the Aswan dam was built, certain historical and natural treasures were relocated. If the Potomac were to be dammed and Washington, D.C. were no longer inhabited, what would you try to save?

Greece

1. If the geography of Greece had been different, for example, a flat, fertile, and united land mass, how might the civilization have developed differently?
2. Given a list of advancements made by the Greeks, identify their major influences on today's society in terms of modern day equivalents or outcomes.
3. Would you have preferred to live in Sparta or Athens? Why?
4. What factors led to the growth of trade in Greek civilization? Why here and not in other early cultures?

5. Compare and contrast the role of verbal and printed means of presenting a political candidate then and now. Consider the role of debates, TV advertizing, bulk mailings, etc.
6. Compare the importance placed on beauty in everyday life in ancient Greece and in modern America. Which was/is more important—form or beauty?

Rome

1. Is geographical expansion good or bad for a society? Look at Rome, European exploration and colonization, United States western expansion, and make a case one way or the other.
2. Given a list of advancements made by the Romans, identify major influences on today's society such as modern day equivalents or outcomes.
3. What procedures need to be standardized in order to promote trade?
4. The Roman Empire expanded to include Great Britain, France, Spain, etc. How was their influence maintained? Is there a similarity to the worldwide spread of American culture?
5. Identify the pros and cons of central and local authority. What should be controlled at each level?
6. While the Roman Empire did not survive as a whole, which of its characteristics are reflected in modern day life?

The class group discussions which follow individual student research and preparation serve as a forum in which students can evaluate and further develop their own thinking patterns. Moreover, the STEP program builds on the introductory experiences which have been a part of those required by activities described throughout this book.

Higher order, or critical, thinking skills tend to be divided into categories for instructional purposes. These include problem solving, decision making, recognizing and using inferences, examination and creation of divergent thought patterns, evaluative thinking, and ultimately, logical reasoning. When devising teaching/learning opportunities for students, teachers need to match activities to these categories.

Higher order or critical thought is used whenever evaluation is called for. Distinguishing between fact and opinion is one of the simpler kinds of evaluation, but to be able to achieve this skill, first the student must learn to identify facts. For this reason, exercises calling for the identification of facts are well-suited to the earliest levels of school library media center and materials usage.

Judging the credibility of a source is for later consideration, but even a very young student can begin evaluating a source by determining how much material is included on a given topic and how many extra features such as pictures, charts or maps are included.

Classifying data is also an evaluative thinking skill. For example, the suggested visit to a church or cathedral to identify architectural features learned about in a book requires some classification. Looking at roofs and photographing specific features also requires classification, as does assigning the sections of the orchestra to which specific musical instruments belong.

Demonstrating sequential order is also an aspect of evaluative thought. Webbing, flow charting, and outlining all require the identification of sequential relationships. So does the creation of timelines.

Evaluating individuals' contributions calls for comparing and contrasting them in order to rank them. Comparisons must also be made in order to demonstrate the extent to which a state may be seen as a microcosm of the nation as a whole.

Evaluating arguments is an important part of taking a stand and justifying one's position. Identifying stated and unstated reasons ties in with decision making as, for instance, whether one would have elected to stay in England or chosen to come to the Colonies (a STEP question.) Planning alternate strategies is incorporated into developing the simple Tyro story and its flow chart.

Divergent thinking is at the heart of each STEP class forum. Listing attributes of objectives or situations is called for repeatedly. Practice in generating ideas as a group permits individual students to improve the fluency of their thinking (i.e., to generate multiple ideas), the flexibility of their thinking (i.e., to experience a wide range of ideas), to recognize details they may have at first overlooked (i.e., elaboration of ideas), and finally, to experience the formation of original or unique thinking.

When an open-ended problem is posed for the forum (or other assignment or activity practice,) there is the opportunity to try several problem solving approaches. Moving from identification of the problem through clarification of the problem, formulating a hypothesis, formulating appropriate questions to be answered, generating related ideas, formulating alternative solutions, choosing the best solution, applying the solution and monitoring acceptance of it, and finally drawing conclusions: all are potential parts of the STEP program model.

As part of the decision-making process, the students will have stated desired goals or conditions, and obstacles to those goals or conditions. They will have identified alternative options, examined those options, ranked them, and chosen what they believe to be the best option—which will then be evaluated.

Gradually, experiences with inductive and deductive thinking (and reasoning) will be presented. The initial foundational parts of these processes can also begin to be presented in bits and pieces at the lowest grade levels. The reading and writing of stories and expository material provides the opportunity to determine cause and effect, analyze open-ended problems, reason by analogy, make inferences, determine relevant information, recognize relationships, and solve insight problems. All of these lead to the final step in the creative thinking process, that of developing new applications and new relationships among ideas or pieces of information.

Opportunities for practice in manipulating information and ideas through thinking—from the specific to the general and from the general to the specific—abound. It is up to the school library media and classroom teachers to see to it that they are seized by the students.

Bibliography

This bibliography is arranged nontraditionally by title to make it easier for the reader to locate bibliographic information about titles referred to in the text. In addition to cited book titles and computer software, the bibliography contains titles of books that have proved useful in various elementary schools that conduct a high level of reference and search practice. These titles are offered only as suggestions to be examined carefully prior to purchase for usefulness in one's own school library media program. The bibliography is *not* intended to be a basic buying list or a mandated collection for carrying out the projects suggested in this book—only a list indicative of the range of materials that have proved useful and supportive of horizon-stretching elementary school reference programs.

Some titles are out-of-print but have been included as examples because they are still found in use in many school and public library collections. The markings J and Y indicate relative school level, with Y extending at times into junior high levels. A few titles marked Adult will be used primarily by teachers, but the content referred to is suitable for, or associated with, J or Y levels. MRDF (machine readable data file) indicates computer software. The initial three digit number is an optional Dewey classification number.

We hope that the specific titles cited in the text and bibliography will spark awareness that elementary grade children can indeed use a broad variety of reference tools effectively. School library media teachers and classroom teachers should be alert to opportunities for using more tools in some of the ways suggested. Young students need all the mind-stretching opportunities they can possibly receive.

523 *365 Starry Nights: An Introduction to Astronomy for Every Night of the Year.* Raymo, Chet. 225 p. Englewood, N.J.: Prentice-Hall, 1982. ISBN 0-13-920512-8   JY

973 *Album of American History.* rev. ed. Adams, James Truslow, ed. 3 vols. New York: Scribner, 1969. ISBN 0-684-16848-0   Y

331 *American Almanac of Jobs and Salaries.* Wright, John. 768 p. New York: Avon, 1982. ISBN 0-380-77933-1   Y

929 *American Badges and Insignia.* Kerrigan, Evans E. 286 p. New York: Viking, 1967. o.p.   JY

394 *American Book of Days.* 3rd ed. Hatch, Jane M., ed. 1212 p. New York: Wilson, 1978. ISBN 0-8242-0593-6   JY

970 *American Indian.* Special ed. for Young Readers. La Farge, Oliver. 213 p. New York: Golden Press, 1960.   JY

929 *American Place Names: A Concise and Selective Dictionary for the Continental United States of America.* 530 p. New York: Oxford University Press, 1970. ISBN 0-19-500121-4   Y

343 *American Political Dictionary.* 7th ed. Plano, Jack C. and Milton Greenberg. 624 p. New York: Holt, 1985. ISBN 0-03-070841-9   Y

973 *American Yesterday.* Sloane, Eric. 123 p. New York: Funk & Wagnalls, 1956. ISBN 0-308-70042-2   Y

599 *Animal Atlas of the World.* Jordan, Emil Leopold. 224 p. Maplewood, N.J.: Hammond, 1969. ISBN 0-8437-1600-2   J

599 *Animals' Who's Who.* Tremain, Ruthven. 335 p. New York: Scribner, 1982. ISBN 0-684-17621-1   JY

MRDF *Answering Questions Library Style.* Greenland, N.H.: Learnco, 1982.   JY

423 *Antonyms: Hot and Cold and Other Words That are as Different as Night and Day.* Hanson, Joan. 32 p. Minneapolis, Minn.: Lerner, 1972. ISBN 0-8225-0276-3   J

709 *Art through the Ages.* 7th ed. De La Croix, Horst and Richard G. Tansey. 922 p. San Diego: Harcourt Brace Jovanovich, 1980. ISBN 0-15-503758-7   Y

925 *Asimov's Biographical Encyclopedia of Science and Technology.* 2nd ed. rev. Asimov, Isaac. 941 p. New York: Doubleday, 1982. ISBN 0-385-17771-2   JY

595 *Audubon Society Field Guide to North American Butterflies.* Pyle, Robert Michael. 917 p. New York: Knopf, 1981. ISBN 0-394-51914-0   JY

595 *Audubon Society Field Guide to North American Insects and Spiders.* Milne, Lorus and Margery Milne. 989 p. New York: Knopf, 1980. ISBN 0-394-50763-0   JY

599 *Audubon Society Field Guide to North American Mammals.* Whitaker, John O. 745 p. New York: Knopf, 1980. ISBN 0-394-50762-2   JY

598 *Audubon Society Field Guide to North American Reptiles and Amphibians.* Behler, John L. and F. Wayne King. 719 p. New York: Knopf, 1979. ISBN 0-394-50824-6   JY

594 *Audubon Society Field Guide to North American Seashells.* Rehder, Harald A. 894 p. New York: Knopf, 1981. ISBN 0-394-51913-2   JY

594 *Audubon Society Field Guide to North American Seashore Creatures.* Meinkoth, Norman A. 766 p. New York: Knopf, 1981. ISBN 0-394-51993-0   JY

910 *Background Notes.* United States Department of State. Bureau of Public Affairs. Approximately sixty notes annually. Washington, D.C.: Government Printing Office. 0-512-161 (48)   Y

927 *Baker's Biographical Dictionary of Musicians.* 6th ed. Baker, Theodore. 262 p. New York: Schirmer, 1978. ISBN 0-02-870240-9   Y

MRDF *Bank Street Writer.* Enhanced version. Bank Street College of Education. San Rafael, Calif.: Broderbund Software, 1984.   JY

808 *Bartlett's Familiar Quotations.* 15th ed. Bartlett, John, comp. 1540 p. Boston: Little, 1980. ISBN 0-316-08275-9   JY

920 *Biography Index.* New York: Wilson, 1966–. Annual.   Y

301 *Black American Reference Book.* Smythe, Mabel M., ed. 1026 p. Englewood, N.J.: Prentice-Hall, 1976. ISBN 0-13-077-386-X   Y

612 *Body Words: A Dictionary of the Human Body, How It Works, and Some of the Things That Affect It.* Daly, Kathleen N. 176 p. New York: Doubleday, 1980. ISBN 0-385-11485-0   JY

394 *Book of Festivals.* Spicer, Dorothy G. 420 p. Detroit: Gale, 1937. Reprint, 1969. ISBN 0-8103-3143-8   JY

030 *Book of Knowledge.* See *New Book of Knowledge.*   JY

200 *Book of Superstitions.* Brown, Raymond L. 116 p. New York: Taplinger, 1970. ISBN 0-8008-0935-1   Y

803 *Brewer's Dictionary of Phrase and Fable.* rev. ed. Brewer, Ebenezer C. 1213 p. New York: Harper, 1981. ISBN 0-06-014903-5   Y

030 *Britannica Junior Encyclopaedia for Boys and Girls.* 15 vols. Chicago: Encyclopaedia Britannica, 1982. ISBN 0-85229-388-7   JY

523 *Cambridge Encyclopaedia of Astronomy.* Milton, Simon, ed. 481 p. New York: Crown, 1977. ISBN 0-517-52806-1   JY

523 *Cambridge Photographic Atlas of the Planets.* Briggs, Geoffrey and Frederick W. Taylor. 224 p. New York: Cambridge University Press, 1982. ISBN 0-521-23976-1   JY

728.8 *Castle.* Macaulay, David. 80 p. Boston: Houghton Mifflin, 1977. ISBN 0-395-25784-0   JY

MRDF *Catalog Card and Label Writer.* Version 4. Bandon, Oreg.: Wehner, 1984.   Adult

MRDF *Catalogit.* PO Box 977, Huntington, N.Y.: Right On Programs, 198–.   JY

726.6 *Cathedral: The Story of Its Construction.* Macaulay, David. 80 p. Boston: Houghton Mifflin, 1973. ISBN 0-395-17513-3   JY

973 *Child Life in Colonial Days.* Earle, Alice Morse. 418 p. Detroit: Gale, 1982. Reprint. ISBN 0-8103-4272-3   JY

016 *Children's Magazine Guide: Subject Index to Children's Magazines.* Sinclair, Patricia Kennelly, ed. Madison, Wis.: Pleasant T. Rowland. vol. 37, 1985.   JY

200 *Christian Book of Why.* McCollister, John C. 337 p. Middle Village, N.Y.: Johnathan David, 1983. ISBN 0-8246-0297-8   JY

903 *Chronology of the Ancient World: 10,000 B.C.–799 A.D.* Mellerish, H. E. L., comp. 500 p. London: Barrie & Jenkins, 1976.   JY

903 *Chronology of the Expanding World 1492–1762.* Williams, Neville, ed. 700 p. New York: McKay, 1969.   JY

903 *Chronology of the Modern World 1763 to Present Day (1965).* Williams, Neville, ed. 937 p. New York: McKay, 1965.   JY

711.4 *City: A Story of Roman Planning and Construction.* Macaulay, David. 112 p. Boston: Houghton Mifflin, 1974. ISBN 0-395-19492-X   JY

973 *Colonial American Craftsmen* series. Fisher, Leonard Everett. 18 vols. New York: Watts.   JY

030 *Columbia Encyclopedia.* See *New Columbia Encyclopedia.*   JY

380 *Complete Junior Encyclopedia of Transportation.* Zehavi, A. M., ed. 280 p. New York: Watts, 1973. ISBN 0-531-02596-9   JY

580 *Complete Trees of North America: Field Guide and Natural History.* Elias, Thomas S. 948 p. New York: Van Nostrand Reinhold, 1980. ISBN 0-442-23862-2   JY

928 *Composers Since 1900: A Biographical and Critical Guide.* Ewen, David, comp. and ed. 639 p. New York: Wilson, 1969.   Y

030 *Compton's Encyclopedia and Fact-Index.* 26 vols. Chicago: F. E. Compton Co., Division of Encyclopaedia Britannica, 1982. ISBN 0-85229-389-5   JY

920 *Concise Dictionary of American Biography.* 3rd ed. 1229 p. New York: Scribner, 1980. ISBN 0-684-16631-3   Y

927 *Contemporary American Composers.* 2nd ed. Anderson, Ruth E. 513 p. Boston: G. K. Hall, 1982. ISBN 0-8161-8223-X   J

920 *Current Biography Yearbooks.* New York: Wilson, 1940–. Annual. ISBN 0-685-30953-3   Y

973 *Diary of an Early American Boy: Noah Blake—1805.* Sloane, Eric. 108 p. New York: Ballantine, 1977. ISBN 0-345-29451-3   Y

920 *Dictionary of American Negro Biography.* Logan, Rayford, W. and Michael Winston, eds. 680 p. New York: Norton, 1982.   JY

580 *Dictionary of Botany.* Little, R. John and C. Eugene Jones. 416 p. New York: Van Nostrand Reinhold, 1980. ISBN 0-442-24169-0   JY

929 *Dictionary of Eponyms.* 2nd ed. Beeching, Cyril Leslie. 160 p. Hamden, Conn.: Shoe String, 1983. ISBN 0-85157-329-0   Y

550 *Dictionary of Geological Terms.* rev. ed. Prepared under the direction of the American Geological Institute. 472 p. New York: Anchor Books, 1976. ISBN 0-385-08425-8   JY

550 *Dictionary of Geology.* 5th ed. Challinor, John. 365 p. New York: Oxford University Press, 1978. ISBN 0-19-520063-2   JY

423 *Dictionary of Homonyms: New Word Patterns.* Ellyson, Louise. 166 p. Mattituck, N.Y.: Amereon, 1979. ISBN 0-88411-136-9   JY

608 *Dictionary of Inventions and Discoveries.* 2nd ed. rev. Carter, Ernest Frank, ed. 208 p. New York: Crane, Russsak, 1976. ISBN 0-8448-0867-9   JY

503 *Dictionary of Named Effects and Laws in Chemistry, Physics, and Mathematics.* 4th ed. Ballentyle, D.W.G. and D. R. Lovett. 346 p. Methuen, N.J.: Chapman & Hall, 1980. ISBN 0-412-22380-5   Y

203 *Dictionary of Saints.* Delaney, John J. 647 p. New York: Doubleday, 1980. ISBN 0-385-13594-7   Y

603 *Dictionary of Space Technology.* Angelo, Joseph A., Jr. 383 p. New York: Facts On File, 1982. ISBN 0-87196-583-6   Y

503 *Dictionary of the History of Science.* Bynum, William F., E. Janet Browne, and Roy Porter, eds. 496 p. Princeton, N.J.: Princeton University Press, 1981. ISBN 0-691-08287-1   Y

423 *Dictionary of the Old West: 1850–1900.* Watts, Peter. 399 p. New York: Knopf, 1977. ISBN 0-394-49013-4   JY

422 *Dictionary of Word and Phrase Origins.* See *Morris Dictionary of Word and Phrase Origins.*   Y

598 *Dinosaur Dictionary.* Glut, Donald F. 218 p. Secaucus, N.J.: Citadel, 1972. ISBN 0-07-035101-5; paper ISBN 0-8065-0283-5   JY

926 *Discoverers.* Grant, Neil. 61 p. New York: Arco, 1981. ISBN 0-668-04784-4   JY

709 *Discovering Art History.* Brommer, Gerald F. 540 p. Worchester, Mass.: Davis, 1981. ISBN 0-87192-121-9   JY

599 *Doomsday Book of Animals: A Natural History of Vanished Spe-*

cies. Day, David. 288 p. New York: Viking, 1981. ISBN 0-670-27987-0   JY

331 *Early Career Books* series. Lerner, Mark, ed. 46 vols. Minneapolis: Lerner, 1980–.   J

973 *Early Settler Life* series. 10 vols. Federal Way, Wash.: Crabtree, 1981–.   JY

550 *Earthquake History of the U.S.* Coffman, Jerry L. and Carl A. Von Hake, eds. 208 p. with 50 p. supplement. Washington, D.C.: Government Printing Office, 1982. SuDoc C55-288:41-1/3. S/N 003-017-00507-1   Y

301 *Ebony Handbook.* Ebony Magazine and Saunders, Doria, eds. 553 p. Chicago: Johnson, 1974. ISBN 0-87485-064-9   Y

420 *Egyptian Hieroglyphs for Everyone.* Scott, Joseph and Lenore Scott. 95 p. New York: Funk & Wagnalls, 1968. ISBN 0-308-80223-3   JY

920 *Eight Black American Inventors.* Hayden, Robert C. 142 p. Reading, Mass.: Addison-Wesley, 1972.   JY

621.3 *Electricity in Your Life.* David, Eugene. 72 p. Englewood, N.J.: Prentice-Hall, 1963.   JY

573.3 *Emergence of Man.* 11 vols. Alexandria, Va.: Time Life, 1974.   Y

916 *Enchantment of Africa* series. Carpenter, Allan. 44 vols. Chicago: Children's Press, 1973–.   JY

917 *Enchantment of America* series. See *New Enchantment of America* series.   JY

030 *Encyclopedia Americana.* 30 vols. Danbury, Conn.: Grolier, 1982. ISBN 0-7172-0111-2   Y

910 *Encyclopedia of Discovery and Exploration.* 18 vols. London: Aldus Books, 1971.   JY

222 *Encyclopedia of Fairies: Hobgoblins, Brownies, Bogies and Other Supernatural Creatures.* Briggs, Katherine M. 481 p. New York: Pantheon, 1978. ISBN 0-394-73467-X   Adult

423 *Encyclopedia of Homonyms: "Sound Alikes."* Newhouse, Dora, comp. 238 p. Los Angeles: Newhouse, 1977. ISBN 0-918050-01-4   JY

608 *Encyclopedia of How It Works from Abacus to Zoom Lens.* Clarke, Donald, ed. 245 p. New York: A. & W. Publishers, 1977. ISBN 0-98479-002-1   J

100 *Encyclopedia of Philosophy.* Edwards, Paul, ed. 4 vols. New York: Macmillan, 1967. Reprint, New York: Free Press, 1973. ISBN 0-02-894950-1   Adult

688 *Encyclopedia of Toys.* King, Constance. 272 p. New York: Crown, 1978. ISBN 0-517-53027-9   JY

391 *Encyclopedia of World Costume.* Yarwood, Doreen. 471 p. New York: Scribner, 1978. ISBN 0-684-15805-1   Y

903 *Encyclopedia of World History: Ancient, Medieval, and Modern, Chronologically Arranged.* 5th ed. Langer, William L., comp. 1569 p. Boston: Houghton Mifflin, 1972. ISBN 0-395-13592-3   Y

300 *Ethnic Almanac.* Bernardo, Stephanie. 560 p. New York: Doubleday, 1981. ISBN 0-385-14144-0   Y

341 *Everyone's United Nations.* 9th ed. New York: United Nations, 1979. ISSN 0071-3244   JY

923 *Facts About the Presidents.* 4th ed. Kane, Joseph Nathan. 464 p. New York: Wilson, 1981. ISBN 0-8242-0612-6   JY

523 *Facts on File Dictionary of Astronomy.* Illingworth, Vallerie, ed. 384 p. New York: Facts On File, 1979. ISBN 0-87196-326-4   JY

574 *Facts on File Dictionary of Biology.* Tootill, Elizabeth, ed. 282 p. New York: Facts on File, 1981. ISBN 0-87196-510-0; paper ISBN 0-87196-637-9   JY

510 *Facts on File Dictionary of Mathematics.* Gibson, Carol, ed. 216 p. New York: Facts On File, 1981. ISBN 0-87196-638-7   Y

703 *Family Encyclopedia of Art.* Myers, Bernard L. and Trewin Copplestone, eds. 320 p. New York: Holt, 1979. ISBN 0-03-049046-4   Y

031 *Famous First Facts: A Record of First Happenings, Discoveries, and Inventions in the U.S.* 4th ed. Kane, Joseph Nathan. 1350 p. New York: Wilson, 1981. ISBN 0-8242-0661-4   JY

016 *Fantasy for Children: An Annotated Checklist.* 2nd ed. Lynn, Ruth Nadelman. 444 p. New York: Bowker, 1983. ISBN 0-8352-1732-9   Adult

394 *Festivals of Western Europe.* Spicer, Dorothy G. 275 p. New York: Wilson, 1958. o.p.   Y

550 *Field Guide to the Atmosphere.* Schaefer, Vincent J., and John A. Day. 359 p. Boston: Houghton Mifflin, 1981. ISBN 0-395-24080-8   JY

598 *Field Guide to the Birds: A Completely New Guide to All the Birds of Eastern and Central North America.* 4th ed. Peterson, Roger Tory. 384 p. Boston: Houghton Mifflin, 1980. ISBN 0-395-26621-1; paper ISBN 0-395-26619-X   JY

928 *Fifth Book of Junior Authors.* Holtze, Sally Holmes, ed. 370 p. New York: Wilson, 1983. ISBN 0-8242-0694-0   JY

394 *First Book of Holidays.* rev. ed. Burnett, Bernice. 87 p. New York: Watts, 1974. ISBN 0-531-00548-8. o.p.   J

030 *First of Everything: A Compendium of Important, Eventful, and Just-plain-fun Facts About All Kinds of Firsts.* Sanders, Dennis. 400 p. New York: Delacorte, 1981. ISBN 0-440-02576-1   JY

391 *Five Centuries of American Costume.* Wilcox, Ruth T. 207 p. New York: Scribner, 1963. ISBN 0-684-15161-8   Y

929 *Flag Book of the United States*. rev. ed. Smith, Whitney. 306 p. New York: Morrow, 1975. ISBN 0-688-02977-9   JY

929 *Flags of the World*. Barraclough, E. M., ed. 264 p. New York: Warne, 1981. ISBN 0-7232-2797-7   JY

580 *Flowers of the World*. Perry, Frances. 320 p. New York: Crown, 1972. ISBN 0-600-01634-X   Y

928 *Fourth Book of Junior Authors and Illustrators*. de Montreville, Doris and Elizabeth D. Crawford, eds. 370 p. New York: Wilson, 1978. ISBN 0-8242-0568-5   JY

300 *Funk and Wagnalls Standard Dictionary of Folklore, Mythology and Legend*. Leach, Maria, ed. 2 vols. New York: Funk & Wagnalls, 1949–50. Reprint, New York: Crowell, 1972. ISBN 0-308-40090-9   JY

703 *Glossary of Art, Architecture, and Design Since 1945*. 2nd ed. Walker, John A. 261 p. Hamden, Conn.: Shoe String, 1977. ISBN 0-208-01543-4   JY

811 *Granger's Index to Poetry*. New York: Columbia University Press, 1904–. (7th ed., 1982). ISBN 0-231-05002-X   Y

703 *Graphic Arts Encyclopedia*. 2nd ed. Stevenson, George A. 483 p. New York: McGraw Hill, 1979. ISBN 0-07-061288-9   Y

923 *Great North American Indians, Profiles in Life and Leadership*. Dockstader, Frederick J. 386 p. New York: Van Nostrand Reinhold, 1977. ISBN 0-442-02148-8   Y

590 *Grolier's Amazing World of Animals*. 20 vols. Danbury, Conn.: Grolier, 1972.   JY

031 *Guinness Book of World Records*. McWhirter, Norris, ed. and comp. 704 p. New York: Bantam, 1984. ISBN 0-553-23990-2   JY

362 *Handbook for the Disabled: Ideas and Inventions for Easier Living*. Lunt, Suzanne. 288 p. New York: Scribner, 1982. ISBN 0-684-17498-7   JY

599 *Harper & Row's Complete Field Guide to North American Wildlife*. Collins, Henry Hill, comp. 2 vols. New York: Harper & Row, 1981. Eastern ed. 714 p. ISBN 0-690-01969-6. Western ed. 809 p. ISBN 0-690-01971-8   JY

310 *Historical Statistics of the U.S.: Colonial Times to 1970*. Bureau of the Census. 2 vols. Washington, D.C.: Government Printing Office, 1976. S/N 003-024-00120-9/ SuDoc C3.134/2:Hb2/970/pt.1-2   Adult

902 *Historical Tables 58 B.C. to 1978*. 10th ed. Steinberg, S. H. 269 p. New York: St. Martin's, 1979. ISBN 0-312-38676-1   Y

709 *History of Art*. 2nd. ed. rev. Janson, Horst W. and Dora J. Janson. 767 p. New York: Abrams, 1977. ISBN 0-8109-1052-7   Y

422 *Hog on Ice and Other Curious Expressions*. Funk, Charles Earle. 214 p. New York: Harper & Row, 1948. ISBN 0-06-001770-8   JY

780 *Home Book of Musical Knowledge.* Ewen, David. 482 p. Englewood Cliffs, N.J.: Prentice Hall, 1954. JY

423 *Homographs: Bow and Bow and Other Words That Look the Same but Sound as Different as Sow and Sow.* Hanson, Joan. 32 p. Minneapolis: Lerner, 1972. ISBN 0-8225-0278-X J

422 *Horsefeathers and Other Curious Words.* Funk, Charles Earle. 240 p. New York: Harper & Row, 1959. JY

603 *How It Works: Illustrated Encyclopedia of Science and Technology.* 20 vols. Freeport, New York: Marshall Cavendish, 1977. ISBN 0-85685-2104 JY

612 *How Things Work Book of the Body.* Amerogen, C. Van. 541 p. New York: Simon & Schuster, 1979. ISBN 0-671-22454-9 JY

422 *I Hear America Talking: An Illustrated Treasury of American Words and Phrases.* Flexner, Stuart Berg. 505 p. New York: Van Nostrand Reinhold, 1976. ISBN 0-442-22413-3 Y

523 *Illustrated Encyclopedia of Astronomy and Space.* Ridpath, Ian, ed. 240 p. New York: Crowell, 1976. ISBN 0-690-01132-6 JY

785 *Illustrated Encyclopedia of Rock.* 3rd ed. 288 p. New York: Harmony, 1982. ISBN 0-517-54661-2; paper ISBN 0-517-53985-3 JY

603 *Illustrated Encyclopedia of Space Technology.* Gatland, Kenneth, et al. 288 p. New York: Harmony, 1981. ISBN 0-517-54258-7 Y

580 *Illustrated Encyclopedia of Succulents.* Rowley, Gordon. 256 p. New York: Crown, 1978. ISBN 0-517-53309-X Y

200 *Illustrated History of the Church.* 12 vols. Minneapolis: Winston, 1980–82. JY

325 *In America* series. 48 vols. Minneapolis: Lerner, nd. JY

016 *Index to Collective Biographies for Young Readers: Elementary and Junior High School Level.* 3rd ed. Silverman, Judith. 405 p. New York: Bowker, 1979. ISBN 0-8352-1132-0 Adult

016 *Index to Free Periodicals.* Rzepecki, Arnold M., ed. Ann Arbor, Mich.: Pierian, 1976–. ISSN 0147:5630 Adult

016 *Index to Poetry for Children and Young People.* Brewton, John E., et al. New York: Wilson, 1972–. Adult

970 *Indians of the Americas.* Sterling, Mather W. 431 p. Washington, D.C.: National Geographic Society, 1955. JY

310 *Information Please Almanac, Atlas and Yearbook.* New York: Simon & Schuster. Annual. ISBN 0-671-25263-1 JY

423 *In Other Words I: A Beginning Thesaurus.* Jenkins, William and Andrew Schiller. 240 p. Glenview, Ill.: Scott Foresman, 1982. ISBN 0-673-12430-4 J

423 *In Other Words II: A Junior Thesaurus.* 3rd ed. Schiller, Andrew

and William Jenkins. 447 p. Glenview, Ill.: Scott Foresman, 1982. ISBN 0-673-12433-9   Y

595 *Insects: A Guide to Familiar American Insects.* Sponsored by the Wildlife Management Institute. Zim, Herbert Spencer and Clarence Cottam. 208 p. New York: Western Publishing, 1951. ISBN 0-307-63504-X   JY

016 *Introducing Books: A Guide for Middle Grades.* Gillespie, John T. and Diana I. Lembo, eds. 318 p. New York: Bowker, 1970. ISBN 0-8352-4115-1   Adult

016 *Introducing More Books: A Guide to the Middle Grades.* Sprit, Diana, ed. 460 p. New York: Bowker, 1978. ISBN 0-8352-0988-1   Adult

917 *In Words and Pictures* series. Fradin, Dennis. 50 vols. Chicago: Children's Press, 1960–.   JY

200 *Jewish Book of Why.* Kolatch, Alfred J. 324 p. Middle Village, N.Y.: Jonathan David, 1981. ISBN 0-8246-0256-0   JY

929 *Jonathan David Dictionary of First Names.* Kolatch, Alfred. 506 p. Middle Village, N.Y.: Jonathan David, 1980. ISBN 0-8246-0234-X   JY

928 *Junior Book of Authors.* 2nd ed. Kunitz, Stanley, and Howard Haycraft, eds. 309 p. New York: Wilson, 1951. ISBN 0-8242-0028-4   JY

016 *Juniorplots: A Book Talk Manual for Teachers and Librarians.* Gillespie, John T., and Diana I. Lembo. 222 p. New York: Bowker, 1967. ISBN 0-8352-9063-9   Adult

790 *Kick the Can and Over 800 Other Active Games and Sports for All Ages.* Hindman, Darwin A. 415 p. Englewood, N.J.: Prentice-Hall, 1978. ISBN 0-13-515163-5   JY

910 *Lands and Peoples.* Shapiro, William, ed. 6 vols. Danbury, Conn.: Grolier, 1983. ISBN 0-7172-8009-8   JY

790 *Language of Sport.* Considine, Tim. 355 p. New York: Facts On File, 1982. ISBN 0-87196-653-0   JY

500 *Let's Discover.* Daniels, Patricia, ed. 16 vols. Milwaukee: Raintree, 1980. ISBN 0-8172-1782-7   JY

917 *Life in America* series. 5 vols. Grand Rapids, Mich.: Fideler, 1952–67.   JY

914 *Life in Europe* series. 10 vols. Grand Rapids, Mich.: Fideler, 1955–64.   JY

914 *Life in Other Lands* series. 7 vols. Grand Rapids, Mich.: Fideler, 1955–64.   JY

927 *Lincoln Library of Sports Champions.* 3rd ed. Santa Rosa, Calif.: Frontier Press, 1981. ISBN 0-912168-07-2   JY

016 *Literature By and About the American Indian: An Annotated Bibliography.* 2nd ed. Stensland, Anna Lee, with contributions by Anne M. Fadum. 382 p. Urbana, Ill.: National Council of Teachers of English, 1979. ISBN 0-8141-2984-6   Adult

641 *Little House Cookbook: Frontier Foods from Laura Ingalls Wilder's Classic Stories.* Walker, Barbara Muhs. 240 p. New York: Harper, 1979. ISBN 0-06-026418-7   JY

574.5 *Living Earth.* 20 vols. Danbury, Conn.: Grolier, 1973.   JY

423 *Longman Dictionary of English Idioms.* Laurence Urdang Associates. 387 p. New York: Longman, 1979. ISBN 0-582-55524-8   Y

503 *Longman Illustrated Science Dictionary.* Godman, Arthur, ed. 256 p. New York: Longman, 1982. ISBN 0-582-55645-7   JY

914 *Looking At* series. 9 vols. Philadelphia: Lippincott, 1970.   JY

758 *Looking at Art: People at Home.* Conner, Patrick. 47 p. New York: Atheneum, 1982. ISBN 0-689-50252-4   JY

909 *Lost Worlds.* Service, Alastair. 201 p. New York: Arco, 1981. ISBN 0-668-05336-4   JY

914 *Macdonald Countries* series. 22 vols. Morristown, N.J.: Silver Burdett. 1975.   JY

MRDF *Magic Slate.* Pleasantville, N.Y.: Sunburst, 1985.   JY

423 *Magic World of Words.* Morris, Christopher G., ed. 255 p. New York: Macmillan, 1977. ISBN 0-02-578770-5   J

303 *Makers of America.* Moquin, Wayne, ed. 10 vols. Chicago: Encyclopaedia Britannica, 1971. ISBN 0-87827-000-0   Y

916 *Man in Africa.* Allen, William. 172 p. Grand Rapids, Mich.: Fideler, 1972.   JY

910 *Maps on File.* Approximately 350 maps in 2 vols. New York: Facts On File, 1981. Annual update. ISBN 0-87196-742-1   JY

703 *McGraw Hill Dictionary of Art.* Myers, Bernard S. and Shirley D. Myers, eds. 5 vols. New York: McGraw Hill, 1969. ISBN 0-07-07924-2   Y

920 *McGraw Hill Encyclopedia of World Biography.* 12 vols. New York: McGraw Hill, 1973. ISBN 0-07-079633-5   Y

030 *Merit Students Encyclopedia.* 20 vols. New York: Macmillan, 1982. ISBN 02-945660-6   JY

428 *MLA Handbook for Writers of Research Papers.* 2nd ed. Gibaldi, Joseph and Walter S. Achtert. 231 p. New York: Modern Language Association of America, 1984. ISBN 0-87353-132-3   Y

426 *Modern Rhyming Dictionary: How to Write Lyrcis; Including a Practical Guide to Lyric Writing for Song Writers and Poets.* Lees, Gene. 360 p. Port Chester, N.Y.: Cherry Lane, 1981. ISBN 0-89524-129-3   JY

928 *More Junior Authors.* Fuller, Muriel, ed. 235 p. New York: Wilson, 1963. ISBN 0-8242-0036-5   JY

016 *More Juniorplots: A Guide for Teachers and Librarians.* Gillespie, John T., ed. 253 p. New York: Bowker, 1977. ISBN 0-8352-1902-2   Adult

422 *Morris Dictionary of Word and Phrase Origins.* Morris, William and Mary Morris. 654 p. New York: Harper, 1977. ISBN 0-06-013058-X   Y

973 *Museum of Early American Tools.* Sloane, Eric. 108 p. New York: Funk & Wagnalls, 1964.   JY

780 *Music Dictionary.* Davis, Marilyn K. 63 p. New York: Doubleday, 1956.   JY

423 *My First Dictionary.* Krensky, Stephen. 342 p. Boston: Houghton Mifflin, 1980. ISBN 0-395-29210-7   J

292 *Mythology* series. 14 vols. London: Paul Hamlyn, 1967–.   JY

914 *My Village In* series. 14 vols. New York: Pantheon, 1964.   JY

910 *National Geographic Index, 1947–1983.* 606 p. Washington, D.C.: National Geographic Society, 1984. ISBN 0-87044-510-3   JY

917 *National Geographic Picture Atlas of Our Fifty States.* 304 p. Washington, D.C.: National Geographic Society, 1980. ISBN 0-87044-216-3   JY

910 *National Geographic Picture Atlas of Our World.* 304 p. Washington, D.C.: National Geographic Society, 1980. ISBN 0-87044-312-7   JY

070 *National Newspaper Index,* 1979–. Los Altos, Calif.: Information Access Corporation, 1979.   Adult (Teacher use at public library)

030 *New Book of Knowledge.* 21 vols. Danbury, Conn.: Grolier, 1983. ISBN 0-7172-0514-2   J

030 *New Columbia Encyclopedia.* 4th ed. 3052 p. New York: Columbia University Press, 1975. ISBN 0-231-03572-1   JY

929 *New Dictionary of Family Names.* Smith, Elsdon C. 570 p. New York: Harper & Row, 1973. ISBN 0-06-013933-1   Y

917 *New Enchantment of America series.* Carpenter, Allan. 50 vols. Chicago: Children's Press, 1979–.   JY

623 *New Encyclopedia of Motor Cars: 1885 to the Present.* 3rd ed. Georgano, G. V., ed. 704 p. New York: Dutton, 1982. ISBN 0-525-93254-2   Y

641 *New Junior Cookbook.* 4th ed. Better Homes and Gardens. 96 p. Des Moines, Ia.: Meredith, 1979. ISBN 0-696-00405-4   J

929 *Nicknames and Sobriquets of U.S. Cities and States.* 3rd ed. Kane, Joseph and Gerald L. Alexander. 456 p. Metuchen, N.J.: Scarecrow, 1979. ISBN 0-8108-1255-X   JY

973 *Nineteenth Century America* series. Fisher, Leonard Everett. 7 vols. New York: Holiday House, 1979–.   JY

292 *North American Indian Mythology.* Burland, Cottie. 141 p. London: Paul Hamlyn, 1973. ISBN 0-600-02368-0. (One of the 14 vol. *Mythology* series).   JY

920 *Notable American Women.* 3 vols. Cambridge, Mass.: Harvard University Press, 1971. ISBN 0-674-62731-8; paper ISBN 0-674-62734-2   Y

920 *Notable American Women: The Modern Period.* 773 p. Cambridge, Mass.: Harvard University Press, 1980. ISBN 0-674-62732-6   Y

016 *Notes From a Different Drummer: A Guide to Juvenile Fiction Portraying the Handicapped.* Baskin, Barbara H. and Karen H. Harris. 375 p. New York: Bowker, 1977. ISBN 0-8352-0978-4   Adult

641 *Nutrition and Health Encyclopedia.* Tver, David F. and Percy Russell. 569 p. New York: Van Nostrand Reinhold, 1981. ISBN 0-442-24859-8   Y

331 *Occupational Outlook Handbook.* vol. 1–. U.S. Bureau of Labor Statistics. Washington, D.C.: Government Printing Office, 1949–. Biennial. S/N 029-001-02651-0 SuDoc L2.3/4:2200/paper   Y

423 *-Ologies and -Isms: A Thematic Dictionary.* 3rd ed. Urdang, Laurence, ed. 800 p. Detroit: Gale, 1983. ISBN 0-8103-1196-8   Y

599 *Oxford Companion to Animal Behavior.* McFarland, David, ed. 657 p. New York: Oxford University Press, 1982. ISBN 0-19-866120-7   Y

803 *Oxford Companion to Twentieth Century Art.* Osborne, Harold, ed. 655 p. New York: Oxford University Press, 1981. ISBN 0-19-866119-3   Y

808 *Oxford Dictionary of English Proverbs.* 3rd ed. Smith, William George, comp. Rev. by F. P. Wilson. 930 p. New York: Oxford University Press, 1970. ISBN 0-19-869118-1   JY

780 *Oxford Junior Companion to Music.* 2nd ed. Hurd, Michael. 353 p. New York: Oxford University Press, 1979. ISBN 0-19-314302-X   Y

759 *Paintings: How to Look at Great Art.* Campbell, Ann. 136 p. New York: Watts, 1972. ISBN 0-531-01867-9   JY

920 *People Who Made America: A Pictorial Encyclopedia.* 21 vols. Meltzer, Ida S., ed. Skokie, Ill.: U.S. History Society, 1975.   JY

030 *People's Almanac Presents the Book of Lists.* Numbers 1, 2, & 3. Wallace, Irving, et al. 3 vols. New York: Morrow, 1980–83. ISBN 0-688-03574-4   JY

030 *People's Almanac Presents the Book of Predictions.* Wallechinski, David, Amy Wallace and Irving Wallace. 513 p. New York: Morrow, 1980. ISBN 0-688-00024-X   JY

902 *People's Chronology: Year-by-year Record of Human Events from Prehistory to the Present.* Trager, James, ed. 1206 p. New York: Holt, 1979. ISBN 0-23-107811-8   JY

769 *Philatelic Terms Illustrated.* 3rd ed. Bennett, Russell and James Watson, comps. 191 p. Garden City, N.Y.: Stanley Gibbons, 1983. ISBN 0-85259-895-5   JY

523 *Pictorial Guide to the Planets.* 3rd ed. Jackson, Joseph H. and John H. Baumert. 256 p. New York: Harper, 1981. ISBN 0-06-014869-1   JY

422 *Picturesque Expressions: A Thematic Dictionary.* Urdang, Laurence and Nancy LaRoche, eds. 500 p. Detroit: Gale, 1983. ISBN 0-8103-1606-4   JY

371 *Place Called School.* Goodlad, John. 396 p. New York: McGraw Hill, 1983. ISBN 0-07-023626-7   Adult

550 *Planet We Live On: An Illustrated Encyclopedia of the Earth Sciences.* Hurlbut, Cornelius S., ed. 527 p. New York: Abrams, 1976. ISBN 0-8109-0415-2   JY

340 *Political Parties and Civic Action Groups.* Schapsmeier, Edward L. and Frederick H. Schapsmeier. 554 p. Westport, Conn.: Greenwood Press, 1981. ISBN 0-313-21442-5   Y

580 *Popular Encyclopedia of Plants.* Heywood, Vernon H. and Stuart R. Chant, eds. 368 p. New York: Cambridge University Press, 1982. ISBN 0-521-24611-3   JY

932 *Pyramid.* Macaulay, David. 80 p. Boston: Houghton Mifflin, 1982. ISBN 0-395-32121-2   JY

503 *Raintree Illustrated Science Encyclopedia.* 20 vols. Milwaukee: Raintree, 1978.   J

910 *Rand McNally Historical Atlas of the World.* 40 p. Chicago: Rand McNally, 1965.   JY

911 *Reader's Digest Atlas of the Bible.* 256 p. Pleasantville, N.Y.: Reader's Digest Press, 1981. ISBN 0-89577-097-0   Y

599 *Reader's Digest North American Wildlife.* Wernert, Susan J., et al., eds. 576 p. Pleasantville, N.Y.: Reader's Digest Assn. (dist. by New York: Random House), 1982. ISBN 0-89577-102-0   Y

803 *Reader's Encyclopedia.* 2nd ed. Benet, William Rose, ed. 1118 p. New York: Crowell, 1965. ISBN 0-690-67129-8   Y/Adult

030 *Readers' Guide to Periodical Literature.* New York: Wilson, 1900–. Semimonthly, except monthly February, July, and August, with quarterly and permanent bound annual cumulations. ISSN 0034-0464   Y

370 *Realities: Educational Reform in a Learning Society.* A statement

by the American Library Association Task Force on Excellence in Education. 15 p. Chicago: American Library Association, 1984. Adult

200 *Revell's Dictionary of Bible People.* Wright, John Stafford. 239 p. Old Tappan, N.J.: Revell, 1979. ISBN 0-08007-1038-X   Y

973 *Reverence for Wood.* Sloane, Eric. 112 p. New York: Funk & Wagnalls, 1965.   Y

MRDF *Right on Programs.* P.O. Box 977. Huntington, N.Y.: Right On Programs.   JY

423 *Roget's International Thesaurus.* 4th ed. Roget, Peter M., rev. by Robert L. Chapman. 1455 p. New York: Crowell, 1977. ISBN 0-690-00010-3   Y

720 *Roofs Over America.* Downer, Marion. 75 p. New York: Lothrop, Lee & Shepard, 1967.   JY

791.53 *Rooster's Horns.* Young, Ed and Hilary Beckett. 28 p. New York: Collins and World, 1978. ISBN 0-529-05446-9   JY

790 *Rules of the Game: The Complete Illustrated Encyclopedia of all Sports of the World.* Diagram Group. 320 p. New York: Bantam, 1976. ISBN 0-553-01305-7   JY

343 *Safire's Political Dictionary: The New Language of Politics.* Safire, William. 845 p. New York: Ballantine, 1980. ISBN 0-345-28393-7   Y

599 *Sea Guide to Whales of the World: A Complete Guide to the World's Living Whales, Dolphins, and Porpoises.* Watson, Lyall. 302 p. New York: Dutton, 1981. ISBN 0-525-93202-X   JY

920 *Searching for Your Ancestors.* 5th ed. Doane, Gilbert H. and James B. Bell. 212 p. Minneapolis: University of Minnesota Press, 1980. ISBN 0-8166-0934-9   JY

635 *Shelf Pets: How to Take Care of Small Wild Animals.* Ricciuti, Edward. 132 p. New York: Harper & Row, 1972. ISBN 0-6-024993-5   JY

928 *Something About the Author: Facts and Pictures About Contemporary Authors and Illustrators of Books for Young People.* Commaire, Anne. vol. 1–. Detroit: Gale, 1971–. ISBN 0-8103-0071-0   JY

371 *Specific Skill* series. 8 vols. Baldwin, N.Y.: Barnell Loft, 1976.   JY

423 *Spellex Word Finder.* Moore, George. 128 p. Woburn, Mass.: Curriculum Associates, 1975. ISBN 0-89187-133-0   JY

910 *Standard Encyclopedia of the World's Mountains.* Huxley, Anthony, ed. 383 p. New York: Putnam, 1962.   Y

910 *Standard Encyclopedia of the World's Oceans and Islands.* Huxley, Anthony, ed. 383 p. New York: Putnam, 1962.   Y

910 *Standard Encyclopedia of the World's Rivers and Lakes.* Gusswell, Kay, and Anthony Huxley, eds. 384 p. New York: Putnam, 1965.   Y

310 *Statistical Abstract of the United States.* Washington, D.C.: Government Printing Office, 1879–. Annual. S/N 003-024-. ISSN 0081-4741. SuDoc. C3.134:yr   Y

709 *Story of American Art for Young People.* Batterberry, Arlane and Michael Batterberry. 159 p. New York: Pantheon, 1978.   JY

428 *Style Manual for Citing Microform and Non-print Media.* Fleischer, Eugene B. 66 p. Chicago: American Library Association, 1978. ISBN 0-8389-0268-5   Y

016 *Subject Index to Books for Primary Grades.* 3rd ed. Eakin, Mary K. and Eleanor Merritt, comps. 113 p. Chicago: American Library Association, 1967. o.p.   Adult

016 *Subject Index to Poetry for Children and Young People.* Sell, Violet, comp. 1035 p. Chicago: American Library Association, 1977. (rev. 1982) ISBN 0-8486-0013-4   Adult

423 *Suffixes and Other Word-final Elements of English.* Urdang, Laurence, ed. dir., Alexander Humez, ed. 363 p. Detroit: Gale, 1982. ISBN 0-8103-1123-2   Y

500 *Tell Me Why Book* series. Leokum, Arkady. 5 vols. New York: Putnam, 1976.   J

423 *Thereby Hangs a Tale.* Funk, Charles Earle. 303 p. New York: Harper & Row, 1950.   JY

928 *Third Book of Junior Authors.* de Montreville, Doris and Donna Hill, eds. 320 p. New York: Wilson, 1972. ISBN 0-8242-0408-5   JY

902 *Timetables of History.* Grun, Bernard. 676 p. New York: Simon & Schuster, 1979. ISBN 0-671-24988-6   JY

929 *Twentieth-century American Nicknames.* Urdang, Laurence, ed. 398 p. New York: Wilson, 1979. ISBN 0-8242-0642-8   JY

928 *Twentieth-century Children's Writers.* 2nd ed. Kirkpatrick, D.L. 1507 p. New York: St. Martin's, 1983. ISBN 0-312-82414-9   JY

620 *Underground.* Macaulay, David. 112 p. Boston: Houghton Mifflin, 1976. ISBN 0-395-24729-X   JY

016 *United States Government Books.* vol. 1–. U.S. Superintendent of Documents. Washington, D.C.: Government Printing Office, 1982–. Quarterly. Free. ISSN 0734-2764. SuDoc GP3.17/5-. [Must be requested or order placed from previous issue to remain on mailing list (requested each issue).]   Adult

550 *Volcanoes of the World: A Regional Directory, Gazetteer, and Chronology of Volcanism during the Last 10,000 Years.* Simkin, Tom, et al. 232 p. Orlando, Fla.: Academic, 1981. ISBN 0-12-787461-5   JY

608 *Way Things Work: An Encyclopedia of Modern Technology.* New York: Simon & Schuster, 1967–71. vol. 1 ISBN 0-671-22621-5; vol. 2 ISBN 0-671-21086-6   Y

355 *Weapons: An International Encyclopedia from 5000 B.C. to 2000 A.D.* Diagram Group. 320 p. New York: St. Martin's, 1980. ISBN 0-312-85946-5   JY

920 *Webster's New Biographical Dictionary.* 1130 p. Springfield, Mass.: Merriam, 1983. ISBN 0-87779-543-6   JY

903 *Webster's New Geographical Dictionary.* rev. ed. 1568 p. Springfield, Mass.: Merriam, 1980. ISBN 0-87779-446-4   JY

780 *What Instrument Shall I Play?* Ingman, Nicholas and Bernard Brett. 128 p. New York: Taplinger, 1975. ISBN 0-8008-8169-9   JY

423 *What's What: A Visual Glossary of the Physical World.* Bragonier, Reginald, Jr. and David Fisher. 565 p. Maplewood, N.J.: Hammond, 1981. ISBN 0-8437-3329-2   JY

902 *Who Was When? A Dictionary of Contemporaries.* 3rd ed. De Ford, Miriam. 200 p. New York: Wilson, 1976. ISBN 0-8242-0532-4   JY

030 *Who Won What When.* Stuart, Sandra Lee, comp. 488 p. Secaucus, N.J.: Lyle Stuart, 1977. ISBN 0-8184-0247-4   JY

920 *Who's Who in America.* Chicago: Marquis Who's Who, 1899–. Biennial.   Y

927.8 *Who's Who in Rock.* Boon, Michael. 259 p. New York: Everest House, 1981. ISBN 0-89696-184-2   JY

030 *Winners: The Blue Ribbon Encyclopedia of Awards.* Walter, Claire. 750 p. New York: Facts on File, 1978–. Biennial. ISBN 0-87196-368-8   JY

302 *Women's Book of World Records and Achievements.* O'Neill, Lois Decker. 798 p. New York: Doubleday, 1979. ISBN 0-385-12732-4   JY

423 *Word Origins and Their Romantic Stories.* Funk, Wilfred. 432 p. East Brunswick, N.J.: Bell, 1950. ISBN 0-517-26574-5   JY

423 *Words from History.* Asimov, Isaac. 265 p. Boston: Houghton Mifflin, 1968.   JY

423 *Words from Science and the History Behind Them.* Asimov, Isaac. 266 p. Cambridge, Mass.: Riverside Press, 1959.   JY

423 *Words from the Myths.* Asimov, Isaac. 225 p. Boston: Houghton Mifflin, 1961. o.p.   JY

423 *Words on the Map.* Asimov, Isaac. 274 p. Boston: Houghton Mifflin, 1962.   JY

310 *World Almanac and Book of Facts.* New York: Newspaper Enterprise Association, 1868–. Annual.   JY

720 *World Atlas of Architecture*. Norwich, John Julius. 408 p. Boston: G. K. Hall, 1984. ISBN 0-8161-8716-9   JY

030 *World Book Encyclopedia*. rev. ed. 22 vols. Chicago: Field Enterprises, 1983. ISBN 0-7166-0083-8   JY

641 *World Encyclopedia of Food*. Coyle, L. Patrick. 790 p. New York: Facts On File, 1982. ISBN 0-87196-417-1   Y

903 *Worldmark Encyclopedia of the Nations*. 5th ed. Sachs, Moshe Y., ed. 5 vols. New York: Wiley, 1976. ISBN 0-471-74833-1   Y

903 *Worldmark Encyclopedia of the States*. Sachs, Moshe Y., ed. 690 p. New York: Harper, 1981. ISBN 0-06-014733-4   Y

290 *World Mythology* series. 5 vols. New York: Schocken, 1983.   JY

200 *World's Great Religions*. Life Special Edition for Young Readers. Staff of Life, ed. 192 p. New York: Simon & Schuster, 1958. o.p.   J

580 *Yearbook of Agriculture*. United States Department of Agriculture. Washington, D.C.: Government Printing Office. Annual. Selected titles useful such as *Trees* (1949), *Water* (1955), *Food* (1959), and *Seeds* (1961).   Y

792.8 *Young Person's Guide to Ballet*. Streatfeild, Noel. 123 p. New York: Frederick Warne, 1975. ISBN 0-7232-1814-5   Y

Index

Administrators, 16, 99
Allusions, 35
Alphabetizing, two systems of, 32
Annotations, 109
Assignments, small, 97, 152, 154; structure of 90, 99, 101, 128, 151, 158.
Atlas, thematic, 66

Basic curriculum, 4, 5
Basic skills, 5, 10, 33, 104, 159
Bibliographies, 99, 108; style sheet for, 108
Bruner, Jerome, 99

Change, technological and social, 3–6
Checklist, weighting of, 139
Chronologies, 63–64
Cinquain, 39
Classifying, 8. *See also* Skill practice activities: categorizing
Clues from questions, 156
Computers, 92–94
Concordance, 35
Contemporaries, professional, 63–65

Databases, 3, 10, 42
Difficulty levels, 32, 89
Distractors, limiting, 104, 111

Editing process, 132
Environment for learning, *see* Higher Order Intellectual Skills

Equity, 15, 16
Evaluation tools, 8
Evaluative criteria, 139

Fact, definition of, 103
Faculty, evaluation of, 16–17
Flowchart. *See* Organization methods
Footnotes, 99, 108
Foreign language, 33

Gazetteer, 66
Goals statement, 16
Glyphs, 36–37
Government publications, 27
Grading: fairness in, 139; weighting in, 139
Group interaction, 142

Hands-on experience, 18, 41, 98
Higher order intellectual skills: environment conducive to, 14; definition of, 13, 164–66

Independent learning, 97
Indexes: cumulative, 22, 80, 81; multiple, 28, 84. *See also* Periodical indexes
Inference. *See* Thinking skills
Information: types of, 90; use of, 3, 4, 5, 10, 12, 15, 18, 97
Integrated program, 8, 15

Language, changes in, 37

185

Learning process, 98, 101–102. *See also* Assignments

Myths, characteristics of, 40

National reports, 7
Newspapers, 88
Nonfiction, 89; "easy" collection placement of, 42, 90
Note taking: practice sources, 111 passim.; underlining copy, 115

Open approach, 99
Open-ended problems, 142, 159, 160, 165
Organization methods: flowcharting, 128; from general to specific, 123, 125, 166; outlining known information, 125; outlining unknown information, 126; puzzle, 123; relationships, 125; webbing, 126, 150
Outlining. *See* Organization methods

Part to whole, 123, 166
Parts of speech, 38
Peer conferencing, 135
Periodical indexes, 87–88
Periodicals, 82, 87
Plagiarism, 108
Planning cooperatively, 91, 114
Presearch outline, 126
Previewing software, 92, 94
Primary sources, 75, 79, 80
Proofreading, 132
Proverbs, 34

Questions, types of, 160

Reference: materials, types of, 89, 99; process, 11, 101, 102, 145, 154; ready, 27
References, specialized, 32, 41, 66, 77, 80, 89
Reference/non-reference decision, 42, 89
Relationships, fact finding, 123, 125
Research. *See* Reference
Reserve system, 90, 107
Revision process, 132

Roles: of classroom teacher, 11, 13, 14, 101; of school library media center, 14, 17, 101; of school library media teacher, 5, 11, 17, 99. *See also* Teaching

Scheduling, 99
School library media center program, 9, 14, 15, 99. *See also* Roles
Schoolwide activities, 97, 101
Skill practice activities: abbreviations, 21, 31, 36, 64, 72, 85; alphabetizing, 21, 29, 36, 37, 38, 43, 44, 46, 47, 52, 55, 57, 58, 59, 64, 68, 70, 71, 78, 79, 82, 83, 84, 85; alternative terminology, 31, 106; author as subject (by and about), 36; categorizing, 64, 82, 83, 165; charts, interpretation of, 31, 46, 51, 52; chronological arrangement, 28, 36, 48, 49, 64, 85; comparisons, 25; cross-references, 21, 28, 37, 46, 47, 84, 85; cumulative index, 22, 44, 45, 46, 47, 77, 78, 82, 83, 84; fact finding, 21, 23, 24, 30, 71, 83, 103, 165; glossary, 48, 52, 58, 75, 79, 82; illustrations, interpretation of, 22, 47, 49, 51, 56, 76; index, use of, 27, 28, 29, 31, 36, 38, 40, 51, 56, 61, 78; key words, 24, 35, 40, 110, 111, 118; map reading, 51, 66, 67–70, 79; note taking, 21, 46, 83; picture captions, 44, 58, 61, 75, 84; position taking, 141, 159; skimming, 21, 43, 46, 51, 52, 55, 56, 58, 59, 61, 69, 70, 105, 118; sub-headings, 21, 47, 52, 71, 75, 84; symbols, interpretation of, 40, 57, 68, 70, 72, 82; table of contents, use of, 40, 47, 53, 55, 56, 58, 61, 82; textual aids, 28, 36, 64, 98
Skills: hierarchy, 99; integration of, 17. *See* Basic skills
Small groups, 99
Social histories, 62, 74
Standardized tests, 16
Style sheet. *See* Bibliographies
Subject headings. *See* Topic terminologies
Supplements, 81

Teacher: expectations of, 139; influence of, 11. *See also* Roles
Teaching: classroom teacher and school library media teacher as a team, 13, 14, 17, 107, 145, 159; style of, 11–12, 101, 159. *See also* Roles
Thesaurus, 38–39
Thesis statement, 120
Thinking skills, improvement of, 7–8; inference, 137.

Timeline, 50, 55, 64, 77, 157, 165
Topic terminologies, 42, 43, 106
Trade books, 42
Travel guides, 67

Utility disc programs, 94

Webbing. *See* Organization methods
Word book, 34
Worksheets, 18, 98
Writing, relation to thinking skills, 8